AF540555

JOMTEIN DECADE OF EDUCATION

JOMTEIN DECADE OF EDUCATION

Editor
Dr. Digumarti Bhaskara Rao
M.Sc., M.A., M.A., M.Ed., Ph.D.
R.V.R. College of Education
Srivivasa Nagar Colony
Guntur–522006
Andhra Pradesh
India

DISCOVERY PUBLISHING HOUSE
New Delhi

First Published-2001
Reprint : 2012
ISBN 81-7141-618-7

Published by :
DISCOVERY PUBLISHING HOUSE
4831/24, Ansari Road, Prahlad Street,
Darya Ganj, New Delhi-110002 (INDIA)
☎ : 3279245 • Fax : 91-11-3253475
E-mail : dphtemp@indiatimes.com

Printed at:
Dynamic Printers

CONTENTS

Foreword

Preface

1. **THE STATISTICAL ASSESSMENT** 1

2. **THE EDUCATION FOR ALL YEAR 2000 ASSESSMENT** 5

3. **A DECADE OF EDUCATION** 11

Demand for Education

Early Childhood Education and Care

- Gross enrolment in early childhood development programmes (Indicator 1)
- Percentage of new entrants to Grade 1 who have attended some form of organised early childhood development programme (Indicator 2)

Primary Education

- Access to Primary education: Apparent and net intake rates (Indicator 3 and 4)
- Trends in participation in primary education: Gross and net enrolment ratios (Indicators 5 and 6)
- Internal efficiency of education systems (Indicators 12, 13, 14)

Finance

- Public expenditure on primary education (Indicator 7 and 8)
- Public current expenditure on primary education as a percentage of GNP (Indicator 7a)
- Public current expenditure on primary education per pupil, as a percentage of GNP per capita (Indicator 7b)
- Public expenditure on primary education as a percentage of total public expenditure on education (Indicator 8)

Teacher Qualifications

- Percentage of primary school teachers having the required academic qualifications (Indicator 9)
- Percentage of primary school teachers who are certified to teach according to national standards (Indicator 10)
- The pupil/teacher ratio (Indicator 11)

Literacy

- The elimination of adult illiteracy (Indicator 16/17/18)
- Literacy rate of 15-24 year olds (Indicator 16)
- Adult literacy rate (Indicator 17)
- Literacy gender parity index: Ratio of female to male literacy rates (Indicator 18)

Appendices

- Appendix I: The Six Target Dimensions
- Appendix II: Core EFA Indicators
- Appendix III: Key Terms and Definitions
- Appendix IV: Composition of Regions (a and b)

FOREWORD

Education is a fundamental human right. It has a powerful impact on the possibilities that children have to determine and enhance their futures. This report offers a first insight into the data collected through the Education for All assessment. These data enable us to evaluate the extent which the important goals for education agreed in 1990 have been reached and to identify the significant gaps between these goals and the current situation.

This report provides the opportunity for a review of the education situation and the achievements and challenges facing the quantitative assessment. Nevertheless the picture is incomplete as, despite the progress and the effort already made, some countries have not been able to provide data and others have provided only partial data. In addition, the indicators selected to assess progress were themselves only a subset of the indicators needed to have a complete picture of the current situation.

In spite of these limitations, this report will help ensure that the goals set in Dakar, either new or reaffirmed, are defined in unambiguous terms and are realistic. In order to monitor progress towards these goals, robust systems must be put into place to collect appropriate, recent, timely data which have, and are perceived to have, integrity. Some countries need to be supported in the establishment of such statistical systems and in the development of skills and expertise for both data collection and analysis. This involves using an assessment of the current situation to select appropriate policies, the monitoring and appraisal of change in order to understand how the policies are operating and the adjustment of policies in the light of such evaluation.

It will be necessary in the near future to explore how the range of indicators might be enhanced so as to improve the focus on quality and outcomes of the educational systems and efficiency in the use of resources. The challenge will be to ensure that the data collected are relevant to future developments in education.

Denise Lievesley
Director, UNESCO Institute for Statistics

PREFACE

The Education for All (EFA) 2000 Assessment is the most in-depth evaluation of basic education ever undertaken on a global scale. It takes stock of the current status of education in each country and evaluates the progress that has been achieved during the 1990s since the World Conference on Education for All (Jomtien, Thailand, March 1990). Its goal? To generate vital information on all types of programmes, activities and services that aim to meet the basic learning needs of children, youth and adults.

Since July 1998, some 180 countries have undertaken the assessment. Headed by a national EFA coordinator, national assessment teams have prepared reports outlining the progress towards 'Education for All' as well as pinpointing shortcomings towards that goal since 1990 in each country.

This Document offers a first insight into the quantitative data collected through this assessment, at global, regional and national levels. These data are the basis for evaluating the extent to which the goals for education have been met, ad identifying challenges for the future.

The Document provides an overview of the core EFA indicators, supported by tables and graphs of statistics on education for the eleven EFA regions. It presents a decade of education in six key areas: the demand for education, early childhood programmes, primary education, education finance, teachers and literacy. It also bears witness to the importance of quality, relevant and timely data for assessing the state of education today, and as the basis of sound policy-making in the future.

Grateful thanks are extended to UNESCO, EFA Forum Secretariat and UNESCO Institute for Statistics for reproducing the material in this book from "Education For All Year 2000 Assessment: Statistics Document" which was based on data provided in country reports prepared within the Framework of the Education For All Year 2000 Assessment in the UNESCO Institute for Statistics. Thanks are also extended to all the personnel involved in preparing this document.

D. B. Rao
8 September 2000
International Literacy Day

1

THE STATISTICAL ASSESSMENT

The quantitative data gathered as a key part of the EFA assessment provide a picture of the state of education today and are vital to the evaluation and understanding of the progress which has been achieved. The statistical process dates from the mid-decade conference held in Amman, Jordan in 1996 where it was decided that 18 core indicators would be selected as a basis for the assessment. The indicators were based on the six Jomtien target dimensions (see Appendix I): early childhood care and development, primary education, learning achievement and outcomes, adult literacy, training in essential skills and education for better living. In this report, 17 of these 18 indicators are studied.

An international structure at global, regional and sub-regional levels was created in order to support this activity through the creation of Technical Advisory groups. Within each country, national co-ordinators were appointed to lead EFA assessment groups and technical sub-groups. More than 180 countries around the world participated in the Assessment, and came together in regional and sub-regional meetings.

167 countries submitted their national report to the EFA Forum secretariat, and 114 of these were accompanied by specially prepared electronic data sets. This Statistical Document focuses upon the data from these submissions. Country data are

drawn from these country reports even if they conflict with other data held by the UNESCO Institute for Statistics (US). When global or regional estimates have been made however the data provided by countries as part of the EFA assessment have been supplemented by other data collected from them in the past and held in the UIS database. This is because not all countries were able to supply information on all of the indicators requested for the last decade, and to omit them could have biased the global and regional pictures. More detailed information on the sources of data and the mix of EFA and UIS data is provided in this report in relation to each indicator.

Eleven regional groups were created to facilitate the monitoring of the EFA assessment. All the regional conferences before Dakar as well as the regional frameworks for action were organised according to these groups. It is therefore these groups which have been used in this statistical assessment. However, it is important to take into account the composition of the eleven regions (see Appendix IVa) in the reading of this report, as these regions differ from the regions usually used by UNESCO).

An important aspect of data quality is the number and distribution of countries that supplied data. Bias may result from non-response, if the proportion of countries responding is low or if the countries that responded are different in relevant respects from those that failed to provide information. Since interpretation of the data should be informed by the response rate, tables and graphs in this report have been annotated accordingly.

The amount and quality of data received from countries is very variable according to the indicator concerned. For the indicators on a regular basis by UNESCO, expertise and systems have been developed within countries and the EFA returns built upon this experience. For new indicators coverage was much poorer. This variability has constrained the depth of the analysis which can be conducted and to some extent is reflected in the variable coverage of the individual indicators in this report. In particular the analysis of within country variation in educational provision is limited and this report is able only to give a flavour of what might be learnt from disaggregated data.

There is a fundamental way in which the population data reported here differ from those in the UIS database. The usual practice of the UIS is to collect the education data directly from countries but to utilise them alongside population data drawn from the United Nations Population Division. The EFA approach differed from this in that countries were asked to provide both the education and the related population data. This process has resulted in some substantial differences in population data between the returns from the education ministers of countries and the United Nations estimates (which of course are based on data provided by national statistical agencies). The unresolved differences account for many of the discrepancies between previous UNESCO estimates and those reported as part of the EFA assessment.

The assessment focuses on learning what has been achieved over the decade 1990 to 2000. Unfortunately due to the time consuming nature of data collection nationally and internationally there is a lag before data can be available. It is gratifying that for many countries it has been possible to report data relating to 1998, but where these data are not available 1997 data have been used. Wherever possible the benchmark for the beginning of the decade is 1990 but in some circumstances it has been necessary to substitute 1991 data.

The assessment has been completed over a relatively short time period and without the resources to implement within-country programmes to improve or complete the data. Data collection is not unproblematic especially in countries that have weak statistical infrastructures. Thus it must be accepted that the data contained in this report are of variable quality. However once returns were received from countries, systematic attempts were made to identify inconsistencies, gaps and potentially invalid statistics. A dialogue was initiated by the UIS with the countries (by e-mail and face to face in the regional meetings) to try to correct, confirm or supplement the data. Where countries were not able to resolve quality problems these have been noted and are referenced on the CD ROM. Ensuring comparability of data across countries is difficult given that the provenance of data can differ significantly. In some countries the data are largely drawn from administrative sources, whereas in others survey or census materials have been utilised.

Improving the quality and comparability of data constitute an important on-going challenge beyond Dakar.

2

THE EDUCATION FOR ALL YEAR 2000 ASSESSMENT

In 1990, delegates gathered at the World Conference on Education for All in Jomtien, Thailand, to set the future global agenda for education and literacy. They identified several goals, including universal access to primary education for every child, improved access to early childhood care and development programmes and the reduction of adult illiteracy. And they pledged to reach these goals by the year 2000.

In April 2000, the World Education Forum, in Dakar, Senegal, will assess the progress that has been made. This global exercise is a unique opportunity for countries to take educational stock, and is convened by UNDP, UNESCO, UNFPA, UNICEF and the World Bank. The aim of the Forum is ambitious: to adopt an Agenda for Education in the Twenty-first Century.

More than 180 countries have participated in the exercise, coming together for regional and sub-regional meetings to report on progress and share experiences. The UNESCO Institute for Statistics (UIS) has gathered the data from the EFA country reports and has worked to ensure that they are as complete and accurate as possible. The quantitative data gathered as a key part of the EFA assessment provide a picture of the state of education today and are vital :ot he evaluation and understanding of the progress that has been achieved.

The data gathered by UIS highlight the key issues confronting the worldwide education community. In short, although there are more children going to school than at any time in history and more people can read or write than ever before, there are still 113 million children out of school, 97 per cent of them in the less developed regions and 60 per cent of them girls. While some regions, notably Latin America, the Caribbean and East Asia are on course to achieving universal access to primary education, other parts of the world are slipping behind. The problem is particularly marked in sub-Saharan Africa, with an increase in the number of children not in school. Progress has been sluggish on early childhood care and development across the globe, and has virtually collapsed in some countries of the former Soviet Union. Governments are still, for the most part, spending too little on primary education and the ratio of pupils to teachers is over 50 in a large number of countries. Furthermore, there continues to be a chronic lack of data on such issues, suggesting an urgent need for more concerted efforts in this area.

The present report covers all of these areas, outlining the changes in the provision of early childhood education and care and access to primary education. It examines the wide variations in the financing of primary education, and highlights the situation of over-burdened teachers as they try to work with large classes. It also sets out the progress made on adult literacy, assisted by more people emerging from school with the ability to read and write.

I—THE DEMAND FOR EDUCATION

The absolute numbers of children for whom education is needed affects the resources required. And a country's ability to provide education will also depend on the size of the group of children relative to that of the working population.

Population growth is obviously a major factor in the provision of good quality primary education, with the potential to put a great strain on a country's ability to pay and on educational infrastructure to deliver. In sub-Saharan Africa, for example, there were 24 million more children in 1998 than in 1990. Such large increases in the number of children make the achievement of the Jomtien goals that much harder.

a) Universal access to primary education for every child

On a worldwide scale, the total number of primary pupils rose from just under 600 million to over 680 million over the decade, and the percentage of children in school edged upwards, form 80 per cent to 84 per cent. Since 1990, primary enrolments have increased by an average of 10 million each year, almost twice that recorded in the 1980s. The number of children not in school fell from 127 million to 113 million globally,

While the number of new entrants in the first year of primary education has increased globally, the gains made in the developing world as a whole have been dramatic, rising by 11 per cent since 1990.

However, such positive trends mask strong regional disparities, with several regions far from achieving universal primary education and, in the case of sub-Saharan Africa, actually lagging behind.

Latin America, the Caribbean and East Asia seem to be headed for universal access in the near future. While their net enrolment rates have reached or exceeded 100 per cent, the picture is very different in sub-Saharan Africa, where the net enrolment ratio stands at 60 per cent. Of the 113 million children out-of-school in 1998, 42 million lived in sub-Saharan Africa.

The progress made in South and West Asia has been impressive, with a significant increase in the numbers of children actually in school and a small increase in enrolment ratios. Educational systems have, however, struggled to keep pace with the growth in population. Despite a slight reduction in the number of out-of-school children, there are still 47 million children in the region who do not attend school.

The less developed regions as a whole account for 97 per cent of the 113 million children not in school. While there has been a slight improvement in the gap between the enrolment of girls and boys, there are more boys in school in almost every region. Girls still account of 67 million of the children who are not in school, around 60 per cent of the total.

b) Expansion of early childhood care and developmental activities

There has been only minimal progress in this area, with the number of children enrolled in such programmes rising from 99 million in 1990 to just 104 million in 1998-a rise of only 5 per cent. While gross enrolment ratios in the less developed countries remain weak, they have fallen fairly dramatically in some of the countries in transition, from 62 per cent to 45 per cent, almost halving the number of children being reached-from 21 million children enrolled in 1990 to 11 million in 1998. This is also due to a dramatic decrease in the population at this age.

The numbers enrolled in such programmes have not changed in the more developed regions because of this already large numbers (gross enrolment ratios of 74 per cent in 1998 against 71 per cent in 1990) and only minor changes in the number of the population of the relevant age. Such programmes showed a significant rise in the less developed regions, up from 56 million children in 1990 to 71 million in 1998. However, this increase stems from a weak starting point of only 24 per cent enrolment in 1990, rising to just 32 per cent in 1998, and from the inability to keep pace with the rising pre-school population.

The disparities within regions are immense, however, with a difference of over 70 percentage points between the highest and lowest enrolment rates in every one of the five regions covered. The greatest variations can be seen in sub-Saharan Africa with gross enrolment ratios lower than 1 per cent in Congo to 111 per cent in the Seychelles. However, of the 79 countries that submitted data on this issue, two thirds have experiences an increase in enrolment ratios-and this ranged from less than one percentage point in Belarus to almost 44 percentage points in Haiti.

II—FINANCIAL RESOURCES FOR PRIMARY EDUCATION

Only half of the countries participating in the EFA Assessment submitted data on education finance. Although there were wide variations, the overall results to suggest, however, that countries are giving a higher funding priority to primary education than they did in 1990. The percentage of public expenditure devoted to primary education in relation to GNP has increased in every region except Central Asia and Central and Western Africa, with the median average for all regions ranging from 0.8 per cent to 2.2 per cent in 1990, rising to 1.3 per cent to 2.3 per cent in 1998

Despite these improvements, however, the overall proportion of public expenditure spent by countries on primary education amounted to less than 1.7 per cent of GNP in 1998. One tenth of the countries studied reported spending less than 0.7 per cent, and one tenth more than 3.6 per cent.

III—TEACHING RESOURCES FOR PRIMARY EDUCATION

The number of pupils per teacher varies enormously on a global scale, from a low of 9:1 to a high of 72:1. In 1998, 75 per cent of the countries reporting had pupil/teacher ratios below 37, a small improvement since 1990. At the same time, the number of countries with pupil/teacher ratios above 50 increased slightly, and now represents around 11 per cent of those countries where such data are available. Most of these countries are in Africa, although high ratios were also reported in South and West Asia. The highest ratios are found in Central and Western Africa, where the average (median) pupil/teacher ratio rose from an already high 50 in 1990 to 52 in 1998.

Of the countries examined, half state that at least 90 per cent of their teachers are qualified, and that 75 per cent hold a teaching certificate.

IV—ADULT LITERACY

The number of illiterate adults fell from 895 million in 1990 to 880 million in 1998 and this downward trend has been more marked among women than men. This represents a 5 per cent increase in the number of adults who can read and write since 1990, rising from 75 per cent to 80 per cent. The literacy rates for young people aged 15-24 increased slightly from 84 per cent to 87 per cent between 1990 and 1998.

However, despite the gains made by women in this area, there is still a long way to go in terms of gender equality. In 1990, there were 8 literate females for every 10 males and this rate saw only a slight improvement over the decade.

The results presented in this report provide not only a global overview of the trends in education over the last decade, but also set the baseline for the goals to be achieved in the next.

3

A DECADE OF EDUCATION

DEMAND FOR EDUCATION

A changing world population: global demographic trends

According to the latest revision of population projections made by the United Nations, the world's population numbers 6.1 billion in year 2000 (this is the middle estimate of three scenarios). This figure is significant when compared to the population of the world at the beginning of the last century-1.5 billion. The growth accelerated throughout the first half of the twentieth century and reached a maximum level of 2.1 per cent annum between 1950 and 1970. A gradual slowing since then has resulted in a current rate of increase of 1.3 per cent. The decrease will continue because of the reduction in size of the population of reproductive age and falling fertility rates.

Global demographic trends mask a very great diversity of situations with growth rates of 3 per cent per annum not uncommon in the less developed regions, especially countries in sub-Saharan Africa (Table 3.1). This translates into a rise of 136 million people over the decade in this region of the world alone. The population growth in less developed regions has meant that their share of the world's population has increased. Eight out of ten people currently live in the less developed regions. This proportion will continue to grow because the fertility rates of these regions are higher than those of more developed regions (Table 3.2).

> *The achievements and failures of the past decade with respect to education should be interpreted in the light of the changes to the social, economic and political order. The 1990s have been characterised by tumultuous change-for example by large scale political changes in Central and Eastern Europe, by economic shocks in East Asia, by the AIDS epidemic in sub-Saharan Africa, and by the eruption of new ethnic and religious conflicts across the world. A further important factor which is critical to the interpretation of the educational progress is the changing numbers of the children and their distribution across the world. The absolute numbers of children for whom education is needed affects the resources required but a country's ability to provide the education will also depend on the size of the group of children relative to that of the working population.*

In addition to the large differences between the more and less developed regions, there are important variations between different countries within the less developed regions of the world. Countries in Latin America and the Caribbean have made substantial progress towards population change with an average number of 2.9 children per woman. Countries in Asia, in particular East Asia dominated by large countries such as China, Indonesia and Thailand, have also achieved a fast pace of demographic transition. The overall fertility rate for this region is 3 children per woman. In South Asia demographic changes, although significant, remain less spectacular with fertility levels of 3.5 children per woman. Sub-Saharan Africa has only recently seen decreases in fertility rates and continues to display high fertility rates at around 5.6 births per woman.

Although it is not the only factor that has an impact on population growth rates, (mortality rates and immigration also play a role), the fertility rate obviously is a major determinant in population growth which impacts upon the demand for education because of its effect on the number of children to be accommodated in school. Obviously a substantial growth in the number of children makes the achievement of the goals of Jomtien that much more difficult.

Table 3.1 — Trends in the world's population in millicns by region

	1950	*1990*	*2000*	*2015*
World	2521	5266	6055	7154
More developed regions	812	1148	1188	1214
Less developed regions	1709	4118	4867	5940
Sub-Saharan Africa	164	462	598	836
North America	172	282	310	343
Latin America/Caribbean	167	440	519	631
East Asia/Pacific	866	1818	2034	2291
South/West/Central Asia	506	1255	1507	1857
Arab States/North Africa	76	225	285	387
Europe	570	784	802	808

Source : United Nations (1999). World Population Prospects. The 1998 revision. Medium-variant projections.

Table 3.2 — Some demographic indicators by region 1995-2000

	Total fertility rate	*Infant mortality rate (%)*	*Life expectancy at birth*
More developed regions	1.7	9	75
Less developed regions	3.0	63	63
Sub-Saharan Africa	5.6	97	50
Latin America/Caribbean	2.9	29	71
East Asia/Pacific[1]	3.0	36	69
South/West/Central Asia	3.5	55	65
Arab States/North Africa	4.5	47	66

Source : United Nations (1999). World population prospects. The 1998 revision. [1]Excluding Australia, Japan and New Zealand.

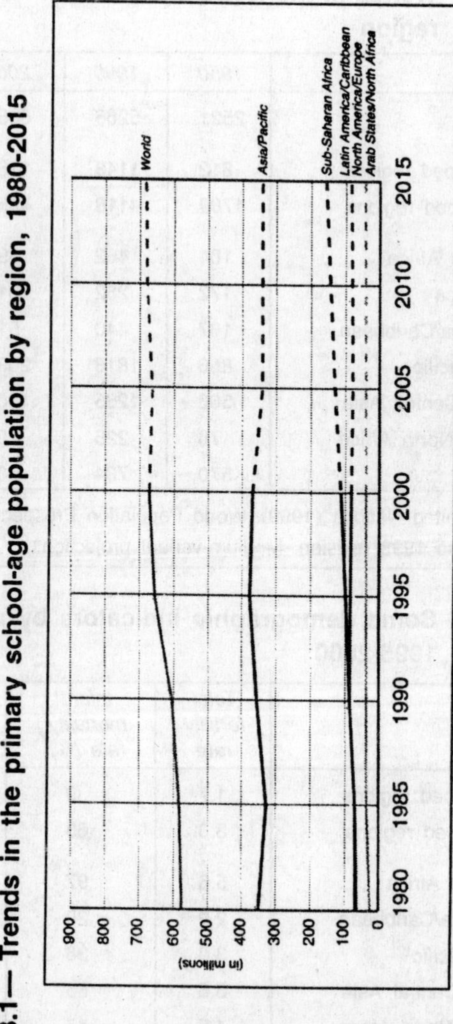

Figure 3.1— Trends in the primary school-age population by region, 1980-2015

Figure 3.2— Trends in the primary school-age population by region, 1980-2015 (index = 100 for 1990

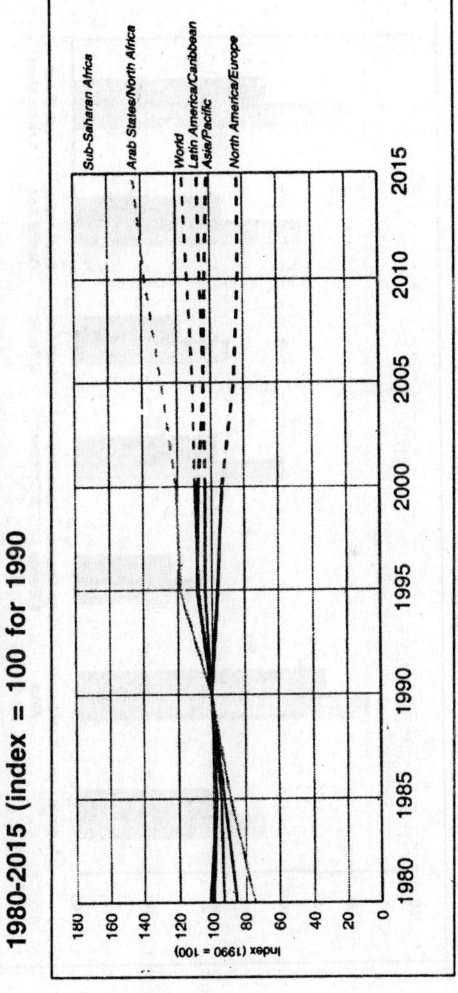

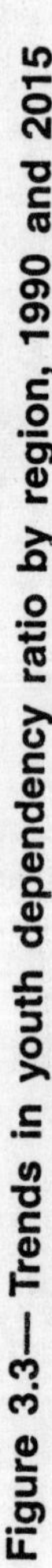

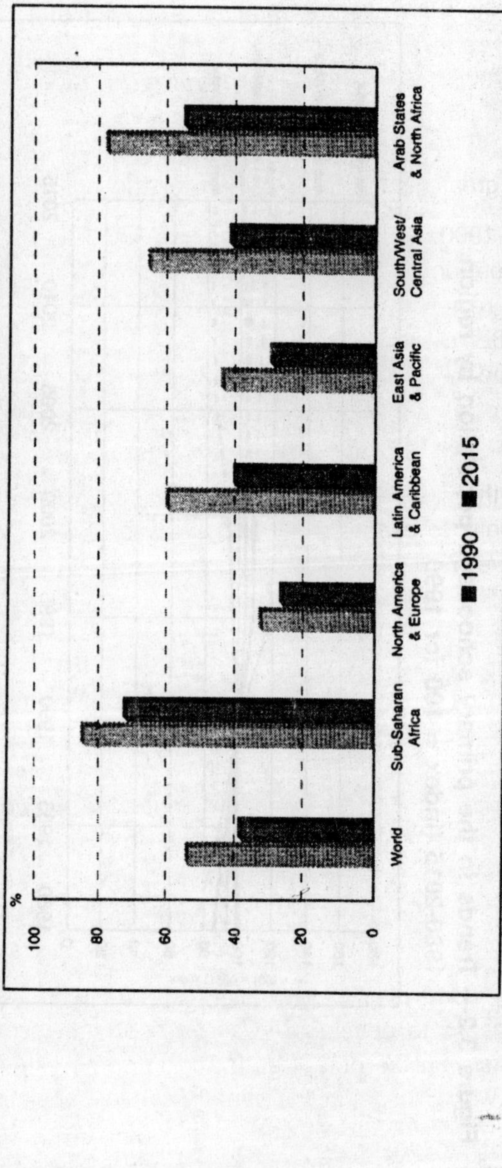

Figure 3.3— Trends in youth dependency ratio by region, 1990 and 2015

Except in North America and Europe where the fall in fertility started much earlier, all the other regions experienced an increase in the number of children of primary school-age. The abrupt reduction in fertility which occurred in Asia has already had visible effects on the size of the school-age population. The primary school-age population in Asia increased only slightly over the decade to 2000 but will fall in the following decades. The number of children of primary school-age is estimated to reach 362 million in 2000 and is projected to decrease to 337 million by 2015. The fall will be greater in East Asia than for the rest of the region.

Since 1990, sub-Saharan Africa has had the second largest population of primary school age children of all the regions in the world. This region recorded a substantial rise in this age group from over 82 million in 1990 and rising to 106 million in 2000. In spite of the deceleration of the rate of increase in the population of children of primary school-age the projection for 2015 is 139 million.

Since the costs of providing education fall on those of working age it is useful to examine the size of the population aged 0-14 years relative to the size of the population aged 15-64 years. All the regions of the world experienced a fall in this ratio over the period since 1990. Not surprisingly the fall is most marked in East Asia and the Pacific where the ratio fell from 46 per cent to 30 per cent and in Latin America and the Caribbean where it fell from 61 per cent to 39 per cent. South, West and Central Asia and the Arab States occupy intermediate positions whereas sub-Saharan Africa is the region where the dependency ratio falls less, from 88 per cent to 72 per cent. (were the population to be evenly distributed across each age group, this ratio would be 30 per cent).

The burden of providing education will remain appreciably high in sub-Saharan Africa beyond 2015 compared with the other parts of the world thus exacerbating the problems in achieving universal access to education in a region where resources are scarce. In Asia on the other hand, and to some extent in other parts of the world, the fall of the primary school population should facilitate the achievement of universal primary education. In countries where all the children of primary age are already in school (China, Indonesia and certain countries of Latin America and the Caribbean as well as developed countries), falling child numbers will make it possible to release resources to improve the quality of primary education and also to develop access to other levels of education.

EARLY CHILDHOOD EDUCATION AND CARE

I—Gross enrolment in early childhood development programmes (Indicator 1)

Response rate[1] : 136 countries

Although countries were asked to report on all early childhood progrommes irrespective of the funding sources, it should be recognised that the sources of information on non-publicly funded programmes can be weak. There are some concerns about the quality of the data relating to early childhood programmes due to difficulties of ensuring that definitions are applied in a comparable way. The definition includes the requirement that, to qualify for inclusion in early childhood development, programmes organised learning activities should form at least 30 per cent of the programme of care. Obviously this requires a sophisticated system of data collection within countries. For these reasons, we would urge caution in the interpretation of some of the data relating to participation in early childhood programmes.

There are an estimated 104 million children enrolled in early childhood programmes (Table 3.3), which is a 5 per cent increase over the 99 million enrolled at the start of the decade. The rise in enrolment was higher in less developed regions-from 56 million to almost 71 million over this period. It is not surprising that the less developed regions saw a greater increase owing to the growth in numbers of young children in this part of the world and the fact that a lower proportion of children were enrolled in early childhood programmes at the start of the decade. The gross enrolment ratios in the more developed regions rose 3 percentage points to 74 per cent during the assessment period. In contrast, gross enrolment in transition countries dropped from 21 million to under 11 million, representing a fall in the rates of children enrolled in early childhood programmes to only 45 per cent. In all regions of the world the proportion of girls enrolled in early childhood programmes rose relative to boys.

The gross enrolment rate for early childhood programmes is calculated by dividing the number of children registered in such programmes by the total number of children in the age-group for which the programmes are designed. The relevant age-group has been specified by each country. If not, it concerns children aged 3 to 5 years. Children outside the relevant early childhood school-age group may attend the programmes and this can result in gross enrolment rates which exceed 100 per cent. This indicator measures the general level of participation of young children in early childhood development programmes. It also indicates a country's capacity to prepare young children for primary education.

The pattern of enrolment in these programmes was extremely variable across the regions both in the levels and the change in levels over time (Fig 3.4). Some regions (Central Asia, and Central and Eastern Europe) showed steep declines in enrolment; others (Latin America and the Caribbean and South and West Asia) showed substantial increases in enrolment levels; the rest of the world experienced more modest increases.

There was remarkable variation of enrolment at the regional level (Fig 3.5) with a difference of over 70 percentage points between the highest and lowest enrolment rates in every one of the five regions shown. The greatest variation occurs in sub-Saharan Africa where gross enrolment ratios range from the Congo with below 1 per cent to the Seychelles with over 111 per cent. Most countries in sub-Saharan Africa have very low rates of enrolment in early childhood programmes as illustrated by the low median of 3 per cent for this region.

Table 3.3 — Number of children enrolled in early childhood programmes and gender disparities, 1990-1998

	Number (in millions)		*Gender parity index*	
	1990	*1998*	*1990*	*1998*
World	99	104	0.84	0.93
More developed regions	22	23	0.88	1.06
Less developed regions	56	71	0.82	0.89
Countries in transition	21	11	0.83	0.98
Sub-Saharan Africa	4	5	0.94	1.13
North America/ Western Europe	20	22	0.84	0.99
Latin America/Caribbean	12	17	0.90	0.92
Central Asia	4	2	0.79	0.88
East Asia/Pacific	31	37	0.85	0.93
South and West Asia	5	8	0.77	0.88
Arab States/North Africa	2	2	0.58	0.85
Central and Eastern Europe	21	12	0.81	0.93

There is wide variation across countries as regards early childhood programmes. The eightly countries which provided data enable us to examine the change in gross enrolment ratios over the assessment period. Of these countries two thirds experienced a rise in their enrolment ratios though the variation in the level of this rise was substantial, ranging from an increase of less than one percentage point in Belarus to almost 44 percentage points in Haiti. Similarly there was substantial variation in the level of decrease amongst the remaining third of the countries with the greatest fall reported by Kazakhastan at 37 percentage points. A number of countries experienced increases or decreases in gross enrolment ratios of more than 15 percentage points between the early 1990s and the latest reported data (Table 3.4).

Figure 3.4— Trends in the gross enrolment ratio in early childhood development programmes by region, 1990-1998

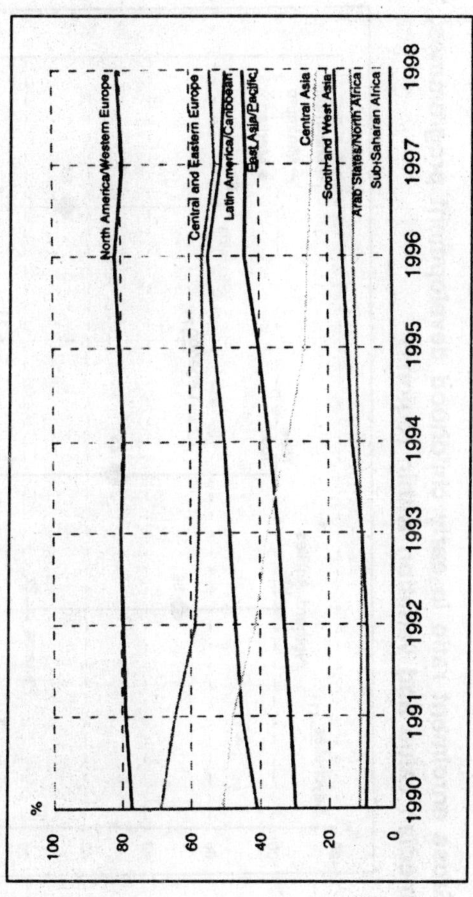

Figure 3.5— Gross enrolment ratio in early childhood development programmes, 1998 (median value and variation within regions)

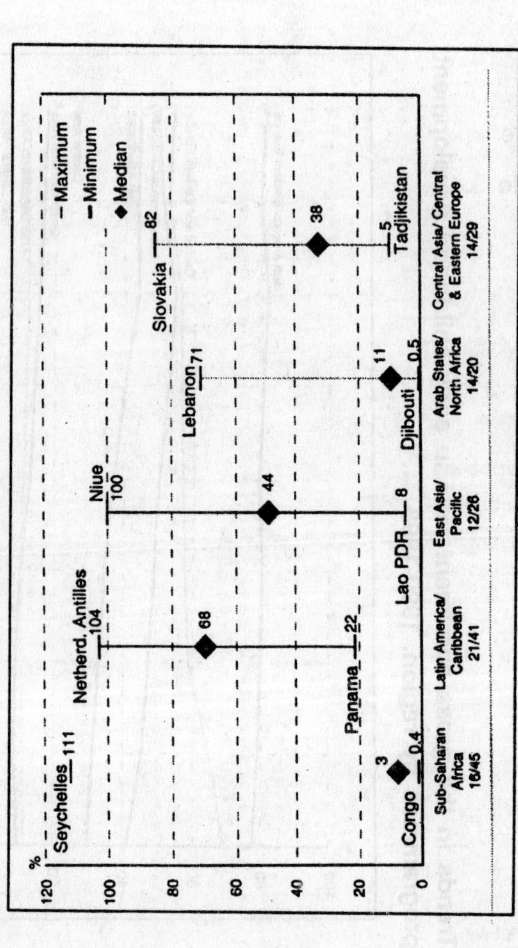

Provincial disparity: Bolivia and Cameroon

A small number of countries provided data which permitted the analysis of education provision within the country. Two such examples demonstrate that national data can mask wide variations in the educational circumstances of children from different areas. There is a persistent discrepancy over the decade in relation to the enrolment of children in early childhood programmes between those in urban and those in rural areas of Bolivia (Fig. 3.6).

Table 3.4 — Gross enrolment ratio in early childhood and development programmes in selected countries, 1990 and 1998

Countries	*1990*	*1998*	*Variation*
Sub-Saharan Africa			
Cape Verde	40	61	21
Equatorial Guinea	14	44	30
Caribbean			
Barbados	53	68	15
Bermuda	133	100	-33
Haiti	21	64	44
Central Asia/Eastern Europe			
Armenia	39	21	-17
Kazakhstan	48	11	-37
Kyrgyzstan	30	8	-22
Lithusania	50	69	19
Ukraine	57	19	-38
East Asia			
China	30	48	18
Malaysia	75	91	16
Thailand	35	69	33

Note : Countries in the table are those which experienced either an increase or a decrease of more than 15 percentage points in the gross enrolment ratio during the period.

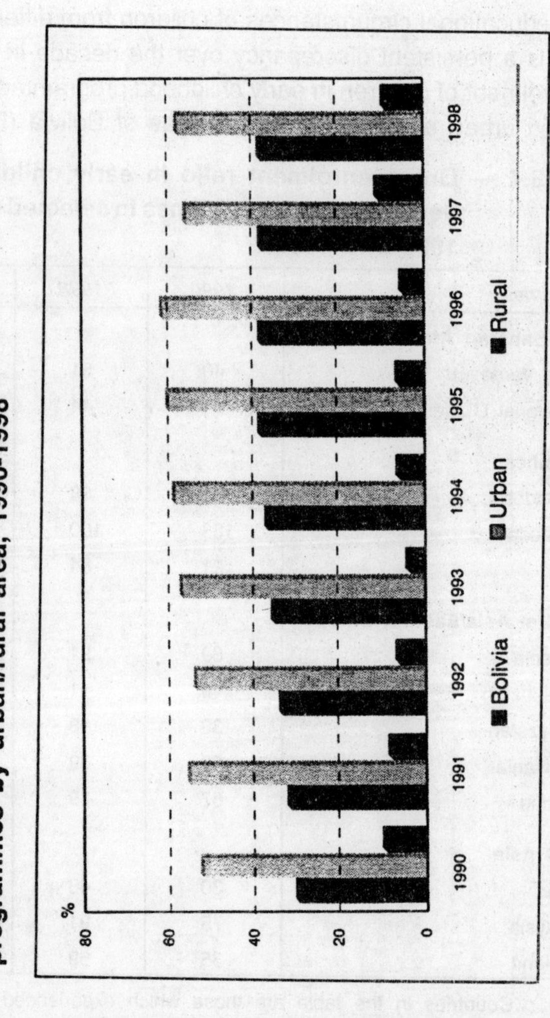

Figure 3.6— Bolivia: Trends in gross enrolment ratio in early childhood development programmes by urban/rural area, 1990-1998

Figure 3.7— Cameroon: Gross enrolment ratio in early childhood development programmes by province, 1990 and 1997

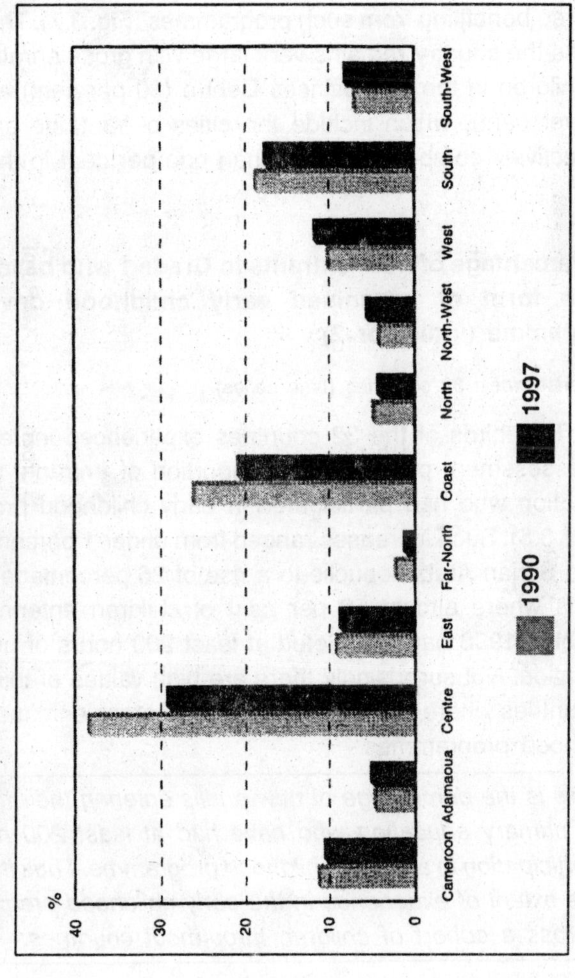

Cameroon data by province also reveal substantial differences in the enrolment of young children in early childhood programmes. Although there is slight evidence of a reduction in these discrepancies between provinces over the seven years, this has been accompanied by an overall small fall in the percentage of children benefiting from such programmes (Fig. 3.7). The variation across the country remains very large with gross enrolment rates for children in the to provinces Centre (30 per cent) and Littoral (21 per cent), which include the cities of Yaounde and Douala respectively compared to less than one per cent in the extreme north.

II—Percentage of new entrants to Grade 1 who have attended some form of organised early childhood development programme (Indicator 2)

Response rate : 32 countries (time series)

Two-thirds of the 32 countries experienced increases over the assessment period in the proportion of entrants to primary education who had participated in early childhood programmes (Table 3.5). Such increases ranged from under 1 percentage point in the Syrian Arab Republic to a rise of 26 percentage points for Bolivia where almost 58 per cent of children entering primary school in 1998 had completed at least 200 hours of pre-primary education. Not surprisingly there are high values of this indicator in countries where there are high levels of gross enrolment in early childhood programmes.

This is the percentage of new pupils entering their first year of primary education who have had at least 200 hours of participation in an early childhood programme. Thus it reflects the extent of experience in the early childhood programmes across a cohort of children throughout countries.

Similarly, countries such as Mexico, Paraguay, Thailand and Viet Nam, which experienced high growth in their early childhood programmes over the decade also saw rises in the number of children entering primary school having benefited from these programmes. Half of the countries which experienced falls in the gross enrolment ratios also reported that fewer children entering primary school had attended only childhood programmes. However a small number of countries reported conflicting data with rises in gross enrolment ratios but falling levels of experience amongst primary entrants (Kyrgyzstan and Sao Tome and Principle) or vice versa (Qatar). This indicates a lag in changes taking effect or more complex patterns of attendance in early childhood programmes.

Table 3.5 — Percentage of new entrants to grade 1 who attended some form of early childhood development programme, 1990 and 1998

Countries with low levels in 1990	*1990*	*1998*	*1990-1998*
Saudi Arabia	11	21	10
Azerbaidjan	23	20	-3
Bahrain	20	43	23
Benin	6	6	0
Bosnia and Herzegovina	8	4	-4
Djibouti	4	3	-1
Jordan	25	38	13
Kyrgyzstan	3	5	2
Libyan Arab Jamahiriya	3	4	1
Paraguay	21	43	22
Sao Tome and Principe	20	22	2
Syrian Arab Republic	7	7	0
Tajikistan	15	8	-7
Togo	4	2	-2
Yemen	3	4	1
Countries with middle or high levels in 1990			
Antigua and Barbuda	84	92	8
Bahamas	100	100	0
Barbadoss	73	89	16
Belarus	94	100	6
Bolivia	32	58	26

Contd.

1	2	3	4
Costa Rica	57	74	17
United Arab Emirates	63	72	9
Ecuador	34	44	10
Kazakhstan	94	20	-74
Morocco	64	70	6
Mexico	73	91	18
Niue	100	100	0
Qatar	50	45	-5
Republic of Korea	56	76	20
Seychelles	100	100	0
Thailand	71	94	23
Viet Nam	55	70	15

PRIMARY EDUCATION

I—Access to Primary Education: Apparent and net intake rates (Indicators 3 and 4)

Response rate[2] : 109 countries for Indicator 3 and 106 countries for Indicator 4.

The absolute number of new entrants to the first grade of primary education has grown steadily since 1990 in all less developed regions (Table 3.6). In these regions taken as a whole, the number of new entrants increased from 106 million in 1990 to 117 million in 1998, a rise of 11 per cent in relative terms. The declines observed in Central and Eastern Europe were partly due to a reduction in the population cohort at the official entry age.

An increase can also be observed in the level of the apparent intake rates in the different regions. In the less developed regions as a whole, the apparent intake rate rose from 106 per cent in 1990 to 112 per cent in 1998. This trend resulted from different regional patterns. Apparent intake rates reached or exceeded 100 per cent in East Asia and the Pacific, South and West Asia and Latin America and the Caribbean, and reflect the potential capacity to accommodate all children of the official entrance age. The rate in sub-Saharan Africa, 81 per cent in 1998, reflects shortcomings in education provision.

The analysis of apparent intake rates by gender in less developed regions suggests that rates were generally higher for boys compared to girls during the period. However, many countries in the East Asia and the Pacific and Latin America and the Caribbean regions had high levels of gender parity.

Apparent intake rates varied widely across the less developed regions, but reflected greater homogeneity in Central Asia and Central and Eastern Europe (Fig. 3.8).

These two indicators measure the level of access to the first year of primary education. The apparent intake rate is based on the total number of new entrants in the first grade of primary education, regardless of age expressed as a percentage of the population at the official primary school entrance age. The net intake rate is based on the number of new entrants in the first grade of primary education who are of the official primary school entrance age, expressed as a percentage of the population of the corresponding age.

Net intake rates for responding countries (Fig. 3.9) shows that the median level of this indicator is 34 per cent in sub-Saharan Africa, 73 per cent in the Arab States and North Africa, 87 per cent in Latin America and the Caribbean, 66 per cent in South and West Asia and 88 per cent in the East Asia and Pacific region. Sub-Saharan Africa is also marked by wide variations in both apparent and net intake rates. Low net intake rates reflect the fact that many children do not enter school at the official age.

The comparison of apparent and net intake rates suggests that a large number of entrants are actually older than the official entrance age. The EFA country reports cited some of the factors underlying late entry into primary education, including economic hardship, paid and unpaid child labour, distance from school and access to transportation. In certain cases, increases in the number of 'older' entrants may be interpreted positively as they result from literacy campaigns, mobilization efforts related to the achievement Education for All goals, or other attempts to stimulate demand for education and to prepare school systems to accommodate children who have already passed the official entrance age.

Table 3.6 — New entrants to first year of primary education by region, 1990 and 1998 (in millions)

Region	1990		1998		Variation
	Total (in millions)	% girls	Total (in millions)	% girls	1990-98 (%)
World	124	46	134	46	8
More developed regions	11	49	11	49	0
Less develpoed regions	106	46	117	46	11
Countries in transition	7	48	6	48	-13
Sub-Saharan Africa	11	46	15	46	40
Latin America/Western Europe	13	49	14	49	10
Central Asia	2	48	2	48	0
East Asia/Pacific	39	47	41	47	4
South and West Asia	38	44	41	44	8
Arab States/North Africa	6	45	6	45	13
Central and Eastern Europe	7	48	6	48	-14

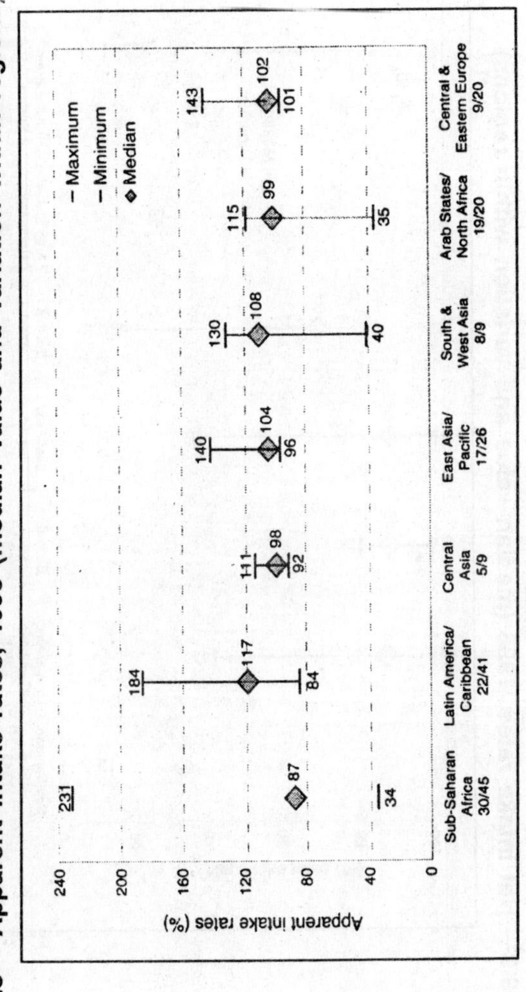

Figure 3.8— Apparent intake rates, 1998 (median value and variation within regions)

Figure 3.9— Net intake rates, 1998 (median value and variation within regions)

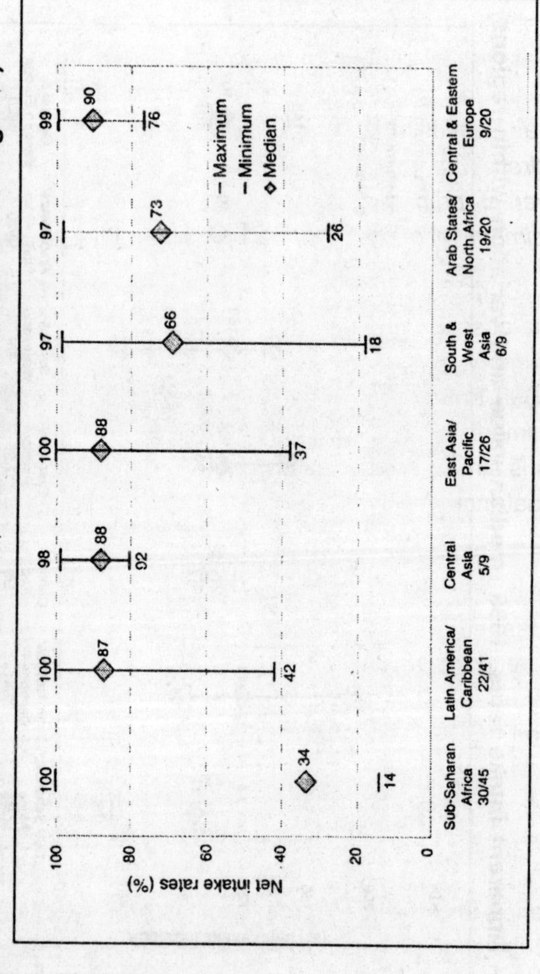

II—Trends in Participation in Primary Education: Gross and net enrolment ratios (Indicators 5 and 6)

Response rate[3]: 142 countries for Indicator 5 and 126 countries for Indicator 6.

Enrolment ratios help to monitor two important issues that are essential to Education for All. First, the gross enrolment ratio can assess whether an educational system has sufficient capacity to meet the needs of universal primary education. Second, the net enrolment ratio shows the proportion of primary school-age children who are enrolled or out of school. The objective of universal primary education implies the realization of a net enrolment ratio equal to 100 per cent.

During the last thirty years, there has been a steady increase in the absolute number of enrolments. The total number of pupils in primary education rose from 411 million in 1970, 599 million in 1990 to 681 million in 1998 (Fig. 3.10). Since 1990, primary enrolments have increased by an average of 10 million each year. This is almost twice that recorded in the 1980s when the average annual increase was about 5.7 million children.

The trend is largely due to progress among the less developed regions, as the more developed regions have largely succeeded in achieving universal primary education. Indeed, for the group of less developed regions, the total number of enrolments grew from 313 million in 1970 to 508 million in 1990 and to 589 million in 1998, accounting for 76 per cent, 83 per cent and 86 per cent of enrolments in the world (Fig. 3.11). Among the less developed regions, the expansion of access to education grew more rapidly than demand, but the rate was not sufficient to achieve universal primary education. In the East Asia, Pacific and Latin America and the Caribbean regions, lower fertility rates greatly contributed to progress towards universal primary education. This was not the case in other less developed regions, where demographic pressures continue to undermine efforts to broaden access to education.

The gross enrolment ratio represents the number of children enrolled in primary education, regardless of age, expressed as a percentage of the eligible official primary school-age population. The net enrolment ratio corresponds to the number of children of the official primary school-age enrolled in primary education expressed as a percentage of the corresponding population.

The positive global trend was accompanied by declining enrolment in some countries. In the case of Liberia, Congo, Sri Lanka, Jamaica and Myanmar, the number of enrolments fell by more than 10 per cent from 1990 to 1998. In certain countries, in particular in East Asia and the Pacific (Thailand, Republic of Korea), Central Asia and Central and Eastern Europe, the decline in enrolments can be explained by a reduction in the size of the school-age cohort as a result of declining birth rates.

Figure 3.10 — Global trends in enrolment numbers in primary education, 1970-1998

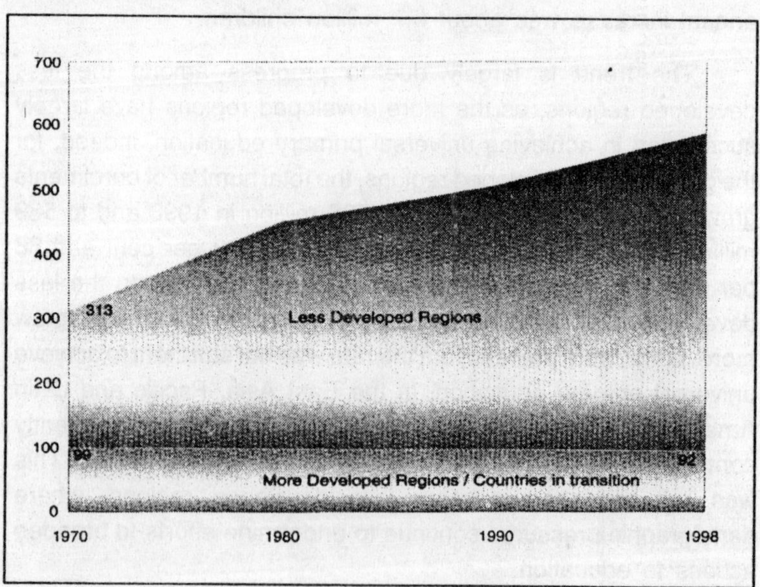

Figure 3.11 — Distribution of primary enrolment numbers by region, 1990 and 1998

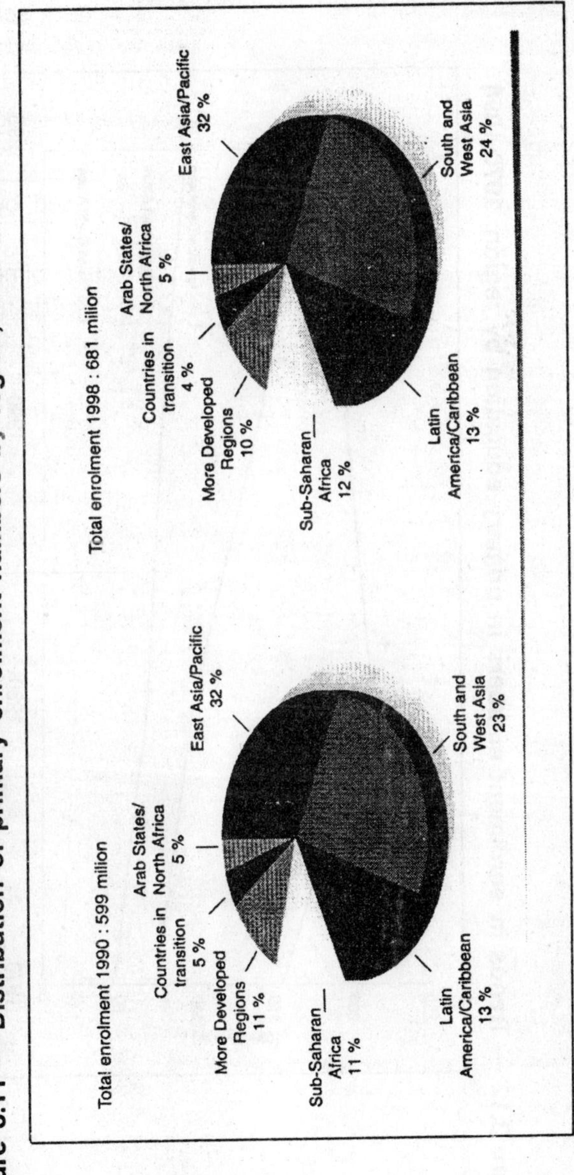

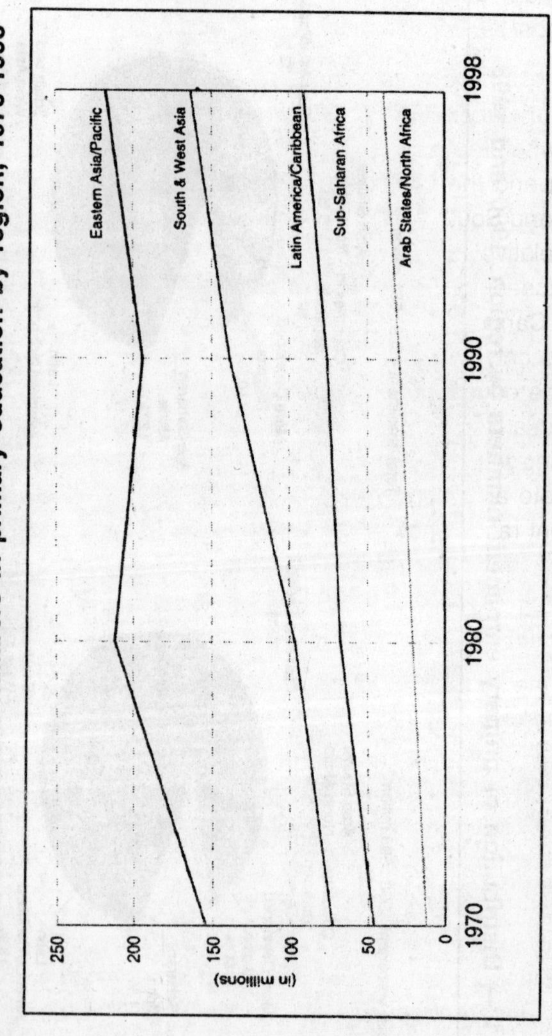

Figure 3.12 — Trends in enrolment numbers in primary education by region, 1970-1998

a) Trends in gross enrolment ratios in primary education

Enrolment and population trends, when translated into terms of enrolment ratios, better situate countries and regions with regard to the goal of universal primary education.

In less developed regions as a whole, the gross enrolment ratio in primary education remained relatively stable during the 1990s, when the ratio grew from 93 per cent to 96 per cent. Latin America and the Caribbean, Central Asia, Central and Eastern Europe and South and West Asia gained at least five percentage points relative to 1990 levels (Fig. 3.13). With gross enrolment ratios exceeding 100 per cent throughout the period. Latin America and the Caribbean and East Asia and the Pacific regions appear to be the only less developed regions with the apparent capacity to provide education for all school-age children. South and West Asia, with a ratio of 91 per cent in 1998, has made some progress in meeting the education needs for school-age children. For the Arab State and North Africa and sub-Saharan Africa, low gross enrolment ratios showed little change over the period. The ratios of 85 per cent in the Arab States and 75 per cent in sub-Saharan Africa reflect continuing difficulties in responding to the potential demand for education which is driven by rapid population growth.

At the same time, in the Arab States and North Africa region three-quarters of the countries had gross enrolment ratios higher than 90 per cent in 1998. However, for some countries in the region, such as Yemen, Sudan, Djibouti and Somalia, the gross enrolment ratios were particularly low or fell during the period. It is important to note that these three latter countries are situated geographically in sub-Saharan Africa where ratios are generally lower.

Only fourteen of the forty-five sub-Saharan African countries (representing 20 per cent of the region's school-age population) have the apparent capacity to provide education for all children. About half of the countries have ratios that are lower than the regional average, i.e. less than 73 per cent. Here, great efforts will be required to guarantee that every school-age child has a place in school.

b) Trends in net enrolment ratios in primary education

The objective of universal primary education implies the realization of a net enrolment ratio equal to 100 per cent.

The East Asia and the Pacific region is close to meeting the goal of universal primary education with a net enrolment ratio of 97 per cent (Fig. 3.14). As this region represents the largest share of the world's school-age population, its high level of enrolment has influenced the global enrolment trend considerably. The Latin America and the Caribbean region showed the greatest growth during the period, with an increase in the net enrolment ratio from 84 per cent in 1990 to nearly 94 per cent in 1998. The level of net enrolment ratios in Central Asia and Central and Eastern Europe (respectively 92 per cent and 93 per cent in 1998) also rose.

In the other less developed regions, net enrolment ratios are still relatively low (below 80 per cent), despite some progress recorded during the decade. The South and West Asia region increased its ratios by seven percentage points, reaching 74 per cent in 1998. In sub-Saharan Africa, the net enrolment ratio grew from 54 per cent in 1990 to 60 per cent in 1998. For the Arab States and North Africa, the net enrolment ratio rose only slightly, by 2 percentage points, to 76 per cent since 1990.

Comparison of gross and net enrolment ratios (Fig. 3.15), indicating the proportion of enrolled pupils not in the official school-age population group, shows that despite a general decline observed between 1990 and 1998, this proportion remains rather large. This is particularly the case in sub-Saharan Africa (20 per cent). South and West Asia (19 per cent) in Latin America and the Caribbean (18 per cent) and in the Arab States and Nort Africa (12 per cent).

Figure 3.13 — Gross enrolment ratio in primary educaiton by region, 1990 and 1998

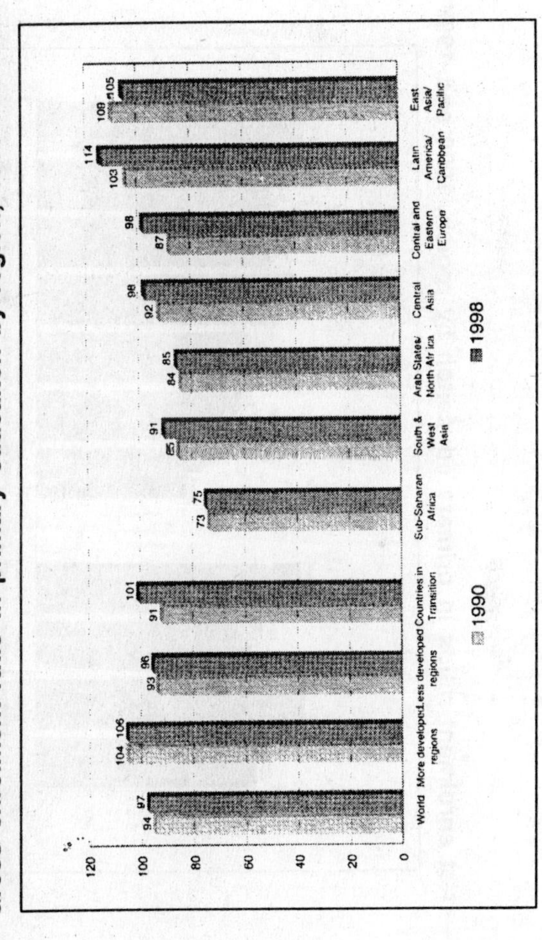

Figure 3.14 — Net enrolment ratios in primary educaiton by region, 1990 and 1998

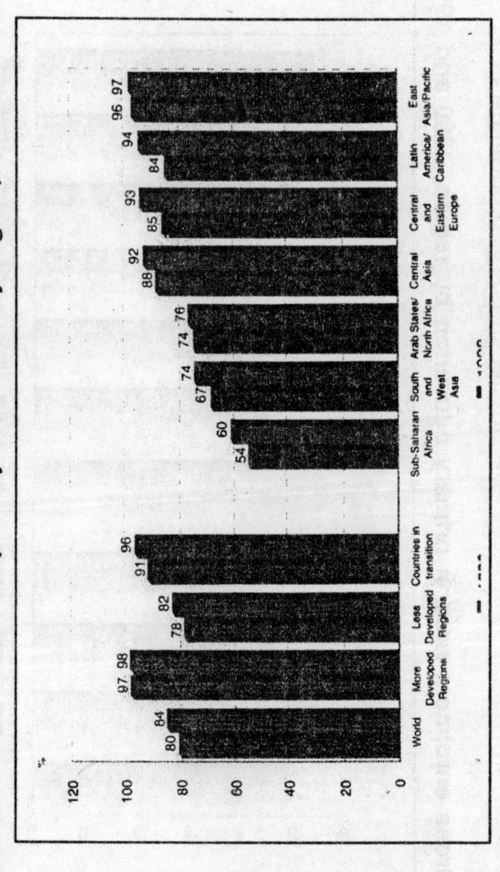

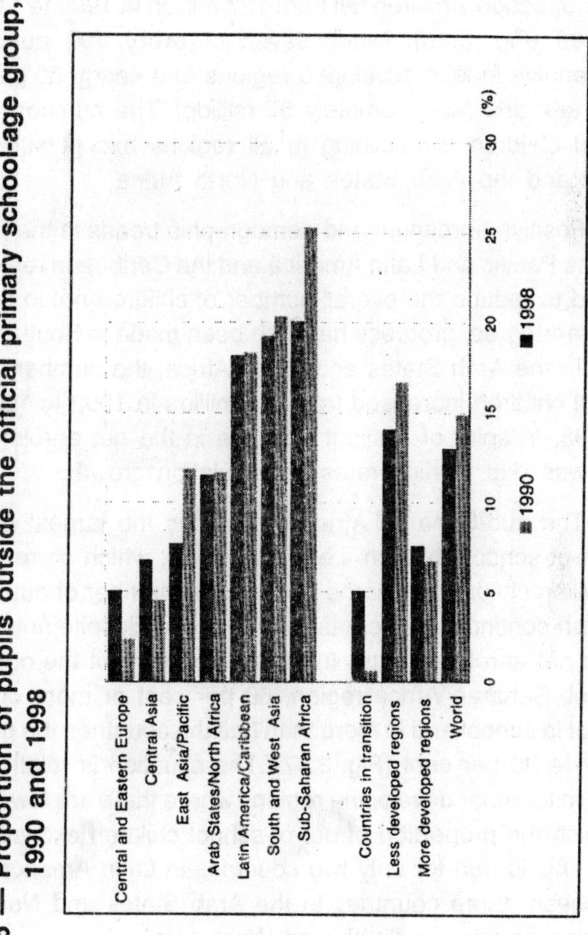

Figure 3.15 — Proportion of pupils outside the official primary school-age group, 1990 and 1998

c) Declining numbers of out-of-school children

The number of out-of-school children is based on the trends in net enrolment ratios and the school-age population.

Based on net enrolment trends, on a global scale the number of out-of-school children fell from 127 million in 1990 to 113 million in 1998 (Fig. 3.16). Ninety-seven of every 100 out-of-school children live in less developed regions and nearly 60 per cent of them are girls (approximately 67 million). The number of out-of-school children is declining in all regions except sub-Saharan Africa and the Arab States and North Africa.

Positive enrolment and demographic trends in the East Asia and the Pacific and Latin America and the Caribbean regions have helped to reduce the overall number of children not in school. To a lesser degree, progress has also been made in South and West Asia. In the Arab States and North Africa, the number of out-of-school children increased from 9.2 million in 1990 to 10.3 million in 1998, in spite of a slight increase in the net enrolment ratio. This was due to high rates of population growth.

The sub-Saharan Africa region has the largest proportion of out-of-school children, i.e. 40 per cent, which corresponds to 42 million children. Over the decade, the number of out-of-school children continues to increase in this region despite notable gains in the net enrolment ratio. In almost one-third of the countries in the sub-Saharan Africa region, 60 per cent or more of children are not in school and in more than half the countries the proportion is above 30 per cent (Fig. 3.17). The situation is relatively more positive for other developing regions where there are few countries in which the proportion of out-of-school children exceeds 30 per cent. This is true for only two countries in Latin America and the Caribbean, three countries in the Arab States and North Africa and one country in South and West Asia.

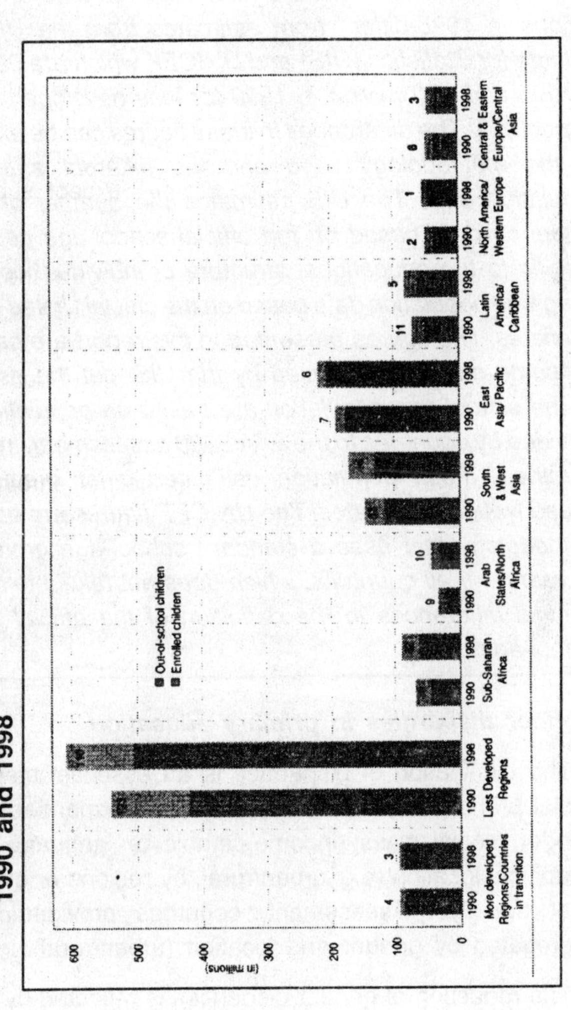

Figure 3.16 — Number of primary school-age children in and out-of-school by region, 1990 and 1998

Accounting for differences in the estimates of out-of-schools children

The number of out-of-school children cited in this report•–113 million for the world and 110 million in less developed regions in 1998-differ from estimates from the UNESCO Institute for Statistics (UIS) and UNICEF which are 93 million in 1995 and 130 million in 1990 for less developed regions respectively. The differences in these figures can be explained by the methodology used and the different sources of population data. The UIS estimates the number of out-of-school children based on the official school-age population specific to the educational structure of individual countries, along with population data based on the official United Nations estimates. The figures presented in this report are based on the same methodology used by the UIS, but the estimates for the school-age population are based on population data provided by countries to the EFA 2000 assessment. In certain countries, these population estimates differ greatly from United Nations estimates. The UNICEF figures are based on methodology that uses a standard school-age group (6 to 11 years) for all countries, which does not take into account national differences in the definition of the official primary school-ages.

d) Gender disparities in primary education

The elimination of disparities is an essential step towards universal primary education. These include disparities according to gender, social class, income, ethnic or language group or geographical location (e.g. urban/rural, by regions or districts). As part of the EFA Assessment, countries provided indicators disaggregated by gender and location (urban/rural).

The reduction of gender disparities is reflected by the gross enrolment ratios. At a global level, the proportion of girl enrolled in primary education, regardless of age, has steadily increased to the point that it almost equals the proportion of girls in the total

Figure 3.17 — Proportions of children in and out-of-school by region and by country, 1998

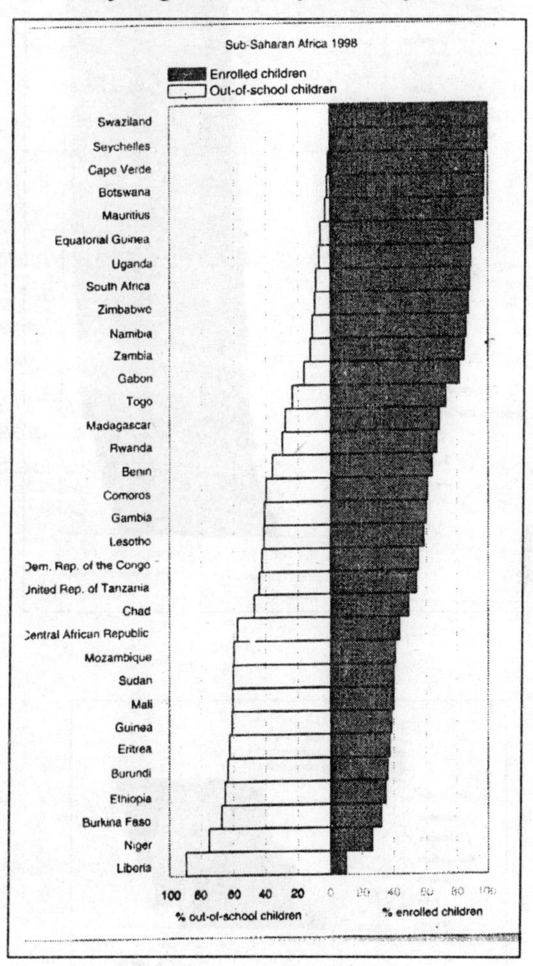

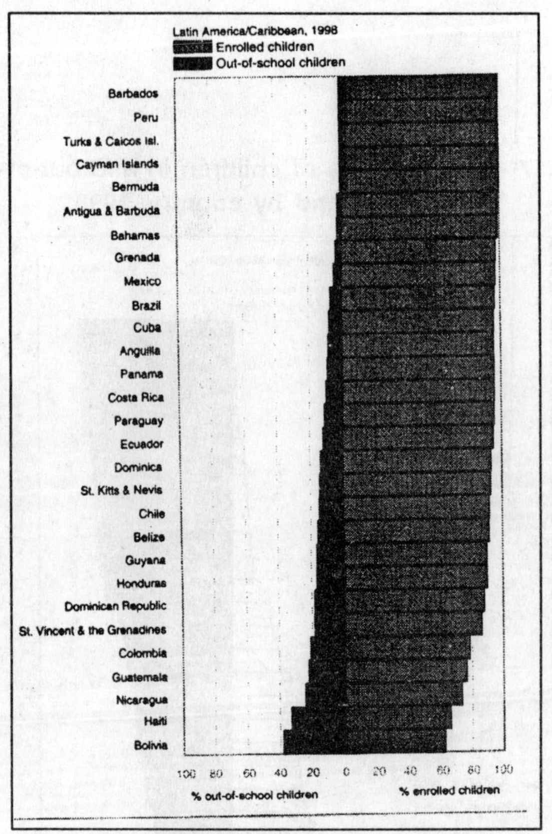
Latin America/Caribbean, 1998
Enrolled children
Out-of-school children
Barbados
Peru
Turks & Caicos Isl.
Cayman Islands
Bermuda
Antigua & Barbuda
Bahamas
Grenada
Mexico
Brazil
Cuba
Anguilla
Panama
Costa Rica
Paraguay
Ecuador
Dominica
St. Kitts & Nevis
Chile
Belize
Guyana
Honduras
Dominican Republic
St. Vincent & the Grenadines
Colombia
Guatemala
Nicaragua
Haiti
Bolivia
100 80 60 40 20 0 20 40 60 80 100
% out-of-school children
% enrolled children

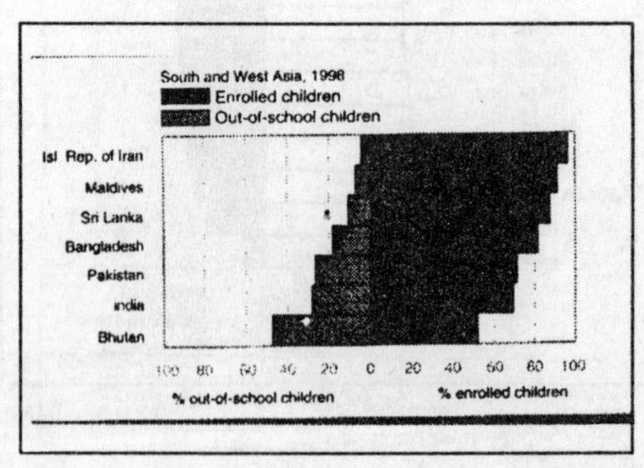
South and West Asia, 1998
Enrolled children
Out-of-school children
Isl Rep. of Iran
Maldives
Sri Lanka
Bangladesh
Pakistan
India
Bhutan
100 80 60 40 20 0 20 40 60 80 100
% out-of-school children
% enrolled children

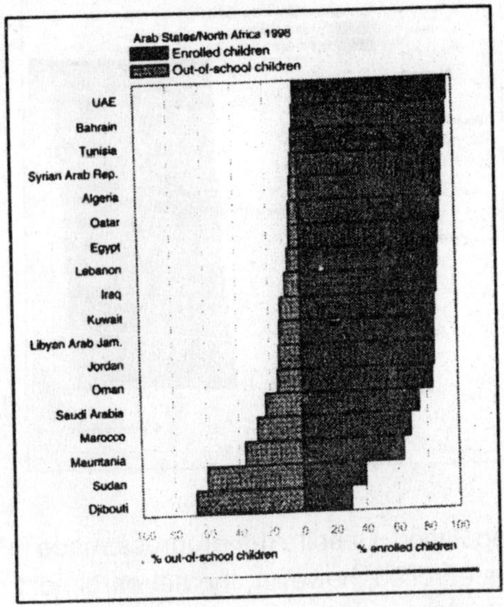
Arab States/North Africa 1998
Enrolled children
Out-of-school children
UAE
Bahrain
Tunisia
Syrian Arab Rep.
Algeria
Qatar
Egypt
Lebanon
Iraq
Kuwait
Libyan Arab Jam.
Jordan
Oman
Saudi Arabia
Marocco
Mauritania
Sudan
Djibouti
0 20 40
% out-of-school children
% enrolled children

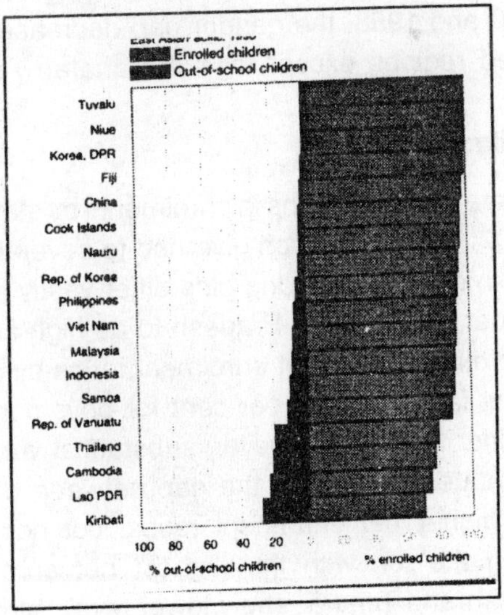
Enrolled children
Out-of-school children
Tuvalu
Niue
Korea, DPR
Fiji
China
Cook Islands
Nauru
Rep. of Korea
Philippines
Viet Nam
Malaysia
Indonesia
Samoa
Rep. of Vanuatu
Thailand
Cambodia
Lao PDR
Kiribati
100 80 60 40 20
% out-of-school children
% enrolled children

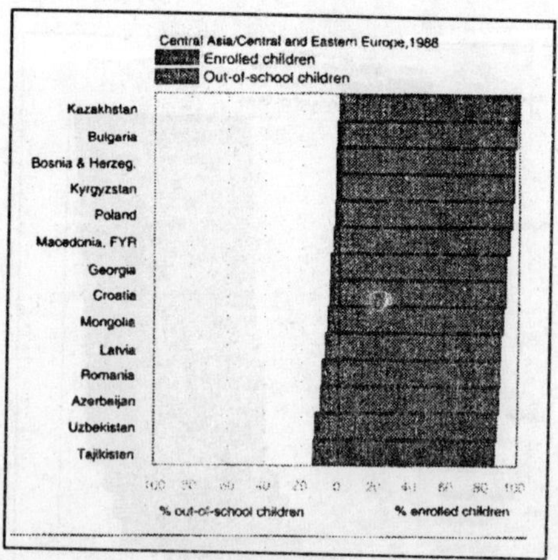

school-age population. Despite the progress made in the absolute number of girls enrolled, however, the net enrolment ratios of girls remain lower than those of boys, especially in sub-Saharan Africa, the Arab States and North Africa, and South and West Asia. This suggests that school-age girls have lower access to primary education compared to boys in the same age-group (Table 3.7). Between 1990 and 1998, the gender gap decreased in all of the less developed regions except for sub-Saharan Africa.

State disparity: India

There were wide variations in enrolments by state and gender in India in 1997 (Fig. 3.8), which give rise to several conclusions. First, net enrolment ratios among girls differ vastly by state, from as low as 36 per cent in Uttar Pradesh to as high as 94 per cent in Assam. The difference in net enrolment ratios by gender at the national level is fairly wide-78 per cent for boys compared to 64 per cent for girls. There is, however, substantial variation among the thirty-two states. Generally, the gap between boys and girls declines with higher net enrolment ratios, but not always. Two regions among the ten with the highest net enrolment ratios, Madhya Pradesh and Tripura, show lower levels of gender parity than other states with lower net enrolment ratios.

Table 3.7 — Net enrolment ratios by sex and gender parity index by region, 1990 and 1998

Region	*1990*			*1998*		
	Boys	*Girls*	*Gender Parity index*	*Boys*	*Girls*	*Gender Parity index*
World	84	76	0.91	87	80	0.93
More developed regions	97	97	1.00	97	98	1.01
Less develpoed regions	82	73	0.89	86	78	0.91
Countries in transition	91	91	1.00	96	96	1.00
Sub-Saharan Africa	59	50	0.84	66	54	0.82
Latin America/Caribbean	85	84	0.99	94	93	0.98
Central Asia	87	89	1.02	91	92	1.01
East Asia/Pacific	97	95	0.98	97	96	0.99
South and West Asia	75	59	0.78	79	67	0.85
Arab States/North Africa	82	65	0.79	80	71	0.89
Central and Eastern Europe	86	83	0.96	95	91	0.96

Table 3.18— India: Net enrolment ratios by gender and by state and territory, 1997

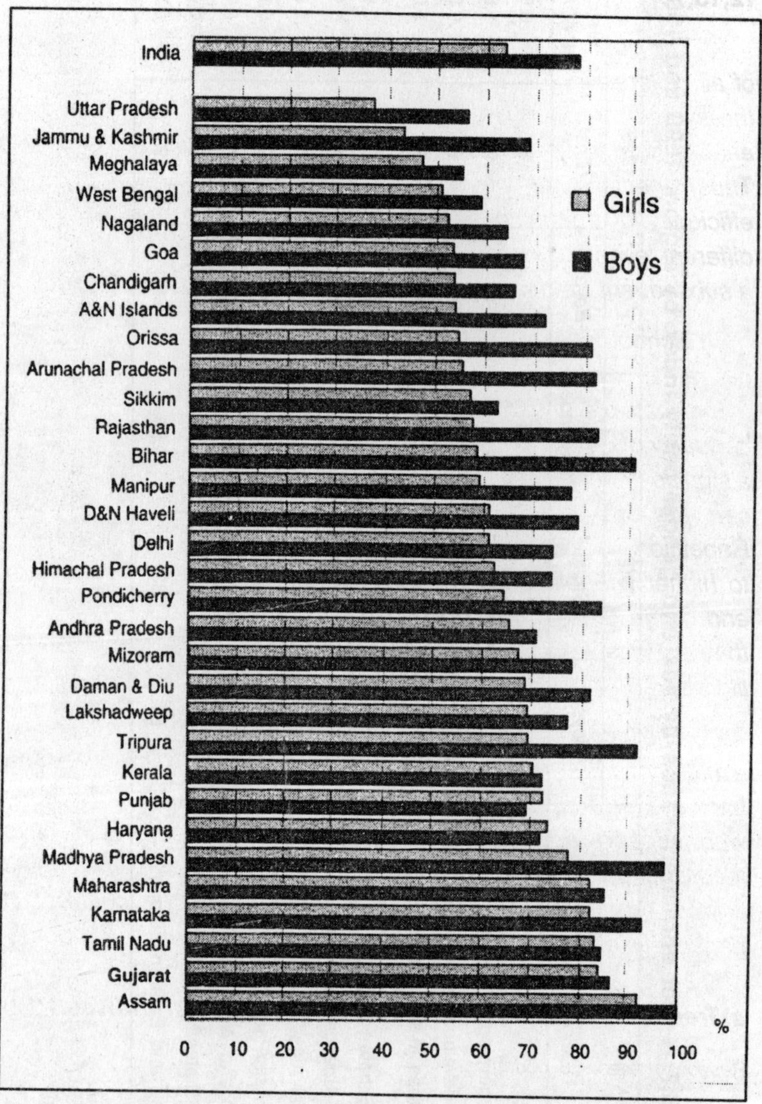

III—Internal Efficiency of Education Systems (Indicators 12,13,14)

The goals of Education for All extend beyond the enrolment of all children in school to ensuring that pupils progress through the system and acquire the basic skills and competencies that enable them to develop personal, citizenship and livelihood skills. Thus, special attention is paid to the analysis of the internal efficiency of education systems, which reflects the dynamic of different 'events' over the school cycle: for example, promotion to a subsequent grade, repetition of a grade, drop-out or graduation.

School 'wastage', which is derived from repetition and drop-out rates, can constitute an important obstacle to the realization of the goals of Education for All. Repetition can be seen as reflexion of quality of education. The inefficient use of school resources has a significant impact as the presence of large numbers of repeaters can prevent other eligible children from accessing schools. Repetition increases the number of pupils per class and thus leads to higher schooling costs. When pupils leave school before the end of the term or the final grade of primary school ('drop-out') they are less likely to have obtained basic competencies, including literacy and numeracy skills.

The advantages or disadvantages of repetition are in fact a matter of debate between those supporting the position of holding back students who have not mastered the curriculum and those who support automatic promotion. Most studies which have focussed on this issue have concluded that repetition doesn't always promote better learning outcomes. On the contrary, it negatively effects pupils who repeat and can lead to dropouts.

a) Trends in repetition rates in primary education (Indicator 12)

Response rate : 36 countries

Between 1990 and 1998 the level of repetition fell in most countries, i.e., in twenty-nine of the thirty-six countries, that provided data (Fig. 3.19). In seven countries, the rate of repetition increased or remained stable. Among those countries where the rate of repetition fell, more than half had an average rate that exceeded 10 per cent in 1998.

The repetition rate measures the proportion of pupils enrolled in a grade in a given school-year who study in the same grade the following school-year. Care should be taken in interpreting this indicator, as a small value may reflect different types of policies: for example, it may reflect the policy of encouraging access without attention to educational quality or it may also reflect highly efficient school system. Conversely, a high repetition rate may reflect high quality standards (in terms of learning achievement) or a high level of inefficiency in a school system.

Despite the general decline, in a number of countries the levels of repetition remain extremely high: nine of the thirty-six countries have an average rate of more than 15 per cent.

b) Trends in survival rates to fifth year of primary education (Indicator 13)

Response rate : 58 countries for 1998, 26 countries (1990 at 1998)

School efficiency, in particular the survival rate, should be analyzed in relation to the level of access (i.e., the intake rates. In fact, a school system may be very efficient in terms of completion rates, but it may admit only a small number of pupils. In this case, the level of observed efficiency relates only to a certain proportion of the school-age children, while a great number of these children are not in school.

The data available indicate that the problem of survival until primary Grade 5 is still a pressing issue in many less developed countries. In certain countries, such as Càmbodia, Colombia, Comoros, India, Lao People's Democratic Republic, Madagascar, Pakistan and Togo, more than 40 per cent of pupils left school before reaching Grade 5 (Fig. 3.20).

Table 3.19— Trends in the average rate of repetition in the first five years of primary education, 1990 and 1998

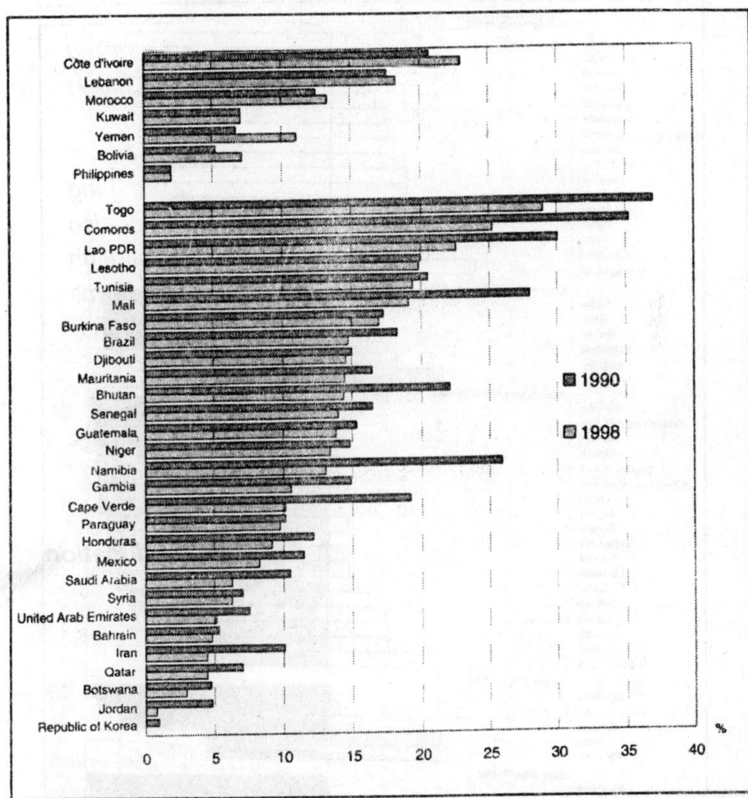

The survival rate to Grade 5 measures the percentage of a cohort of pupils who are enrolled in the first grade of primary education in a given school year and who eventually reach Grade 5. Its purpose is to assess the 'holding power' and internal efficiency of an education system, i.e., the extent to which the system can retain the maximum number of pupils until Grade 5 and therefore avoid early drop-outs. The achievement of five years of primary school has been defined as a minimum requirement for an individual to become literate for life.

Figure 3.20 — Percentage of pupils surviving to Grade 5, 1998

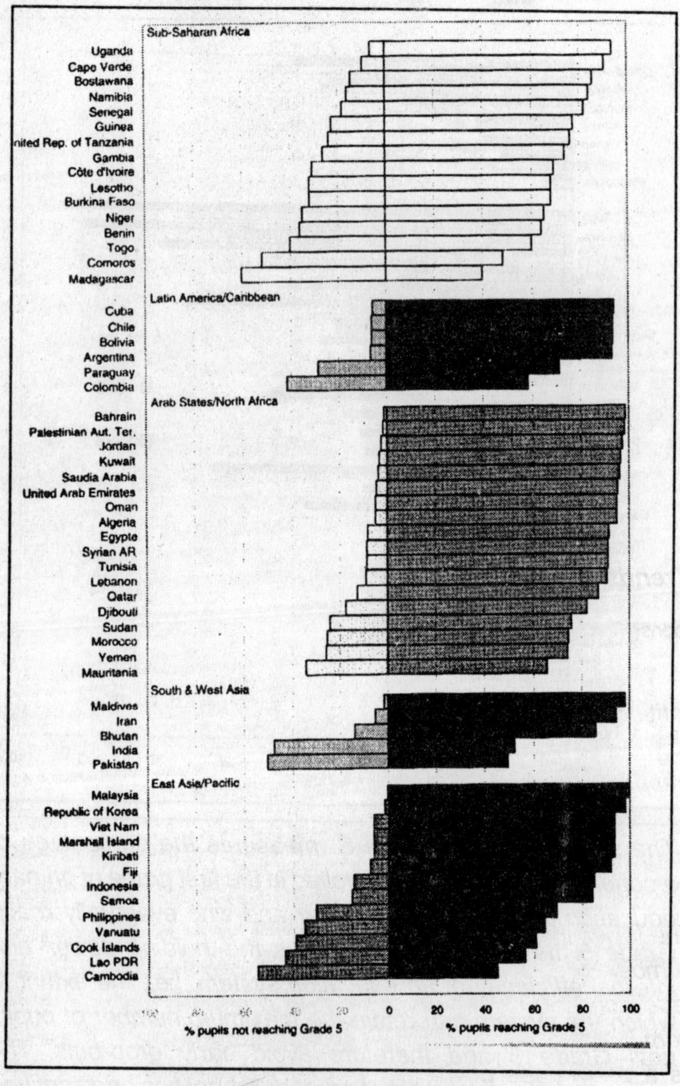

Figure 3.21 — Coefficients of efficiency, 1998 (median values and variation within regions)

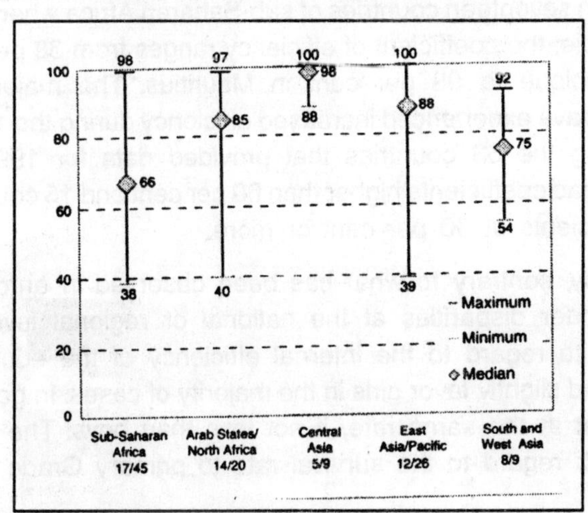

c) Trends in the coefficient of efficiency (Indicator 14)

Response rate : 63 countries for 1998

The coefficient of efficiency reflects the combined impact of repetition and drop-out on the internal efficiency of the school system. The ideal value of the coefficient is 100 per cent, corresponding to a situation where all pupils progress and complete the school cycle, neither repeating nor dropping out. A coefficient that is lower that 100 per cent indicates some level of wastage.

> *The coefficient of efficiency refers to the ideal (optimal) number of pupil-years required (i.e. in the absence of repetition and drop-out) to produce a number of graduates from a given pupil cohort in primary education, expressed as a percentage of the actual number of pupil-years spent to produce the same number of graduates. The coefficient of efficiency is a synthetic indicator of the internal efficiency of an education system.*

There is wide variation in the level of efficiency between countries, even among those in the same region (Fig. 3.21). For instance, in seventeen countries of sub-Saharan Africa where data are available, the coefficient of efficiency ranges from 38 per cent in Mozambique to 98 per cent in Mauritius. The majority of countries have experienced increased efficiency during the 1990s, and among the 63 countries that provided data for 1998, 52 countries had coefficients higher than 60 per cent and 16 countries had coefficients of 90 per cent or more.

Finally, contrary to what has been observed in enrolment ratios, gender disparities at the national or regional level are minimal with regard to the internal efficiency of the education system, and slightly favor girls in the majority of cases. In general, girls repeat at the same rate, if not less than boys. The same is true with regard to the survival rate to primary Grade 5.

FINANCE

Public current expenditure on primary education (Indicators 7 and 8)

All three finance indicators are affected by external factors which can make it difficult to compare countries-especially those in very different circumstances. In particular, thay are dependent on: the duration of the primary phase of education in each country (which in this report varies between 4 and 8 or 9 years between countries); the number of children of school-age in the population-the 'demand' for education-or, at least, the proportion of the demand which is actually met (that is, the actual number of school places provided); the levels of teachers' salaries and other remunerations; the country's ability to 'afford' to pay for education as indicated by the level of GNP per capita and; the level of financial support from private sector which can be large in some countries.

> *This indicator measures public current expenditure on primary education (central, provincial and local) expressed as a percentage of the GNP.*

I—Public current expenditure on primary education as a percentage of GNP (Indicator 7a)

Response rate : 77[4] countries (time series)

Half of the less developed countries which provided data for this indicator reported public spending on primary education of less than 1.7 per cent of their GNP in 1998. One tenth reported spending less than 0.7 per cent and one tenth over 3.6 per cent. The variations reported between regions are quite large although they have narrowed over the asessment period: the median values for each of the nine regions for which data are available were between 0.8 per cent and 2.4 per cent in 1990 and between 1.3 per cent and 2.3 per cent in 1998 (Fig. 3.22).

There are, however, large variations within regions ranging between about 1.5 and 3.5 percentage points between the highest and lowest reported values. Within earch region, these variations are as great or greater than the median value itself. In 1998, the largest variations reported within regions were in Central and Western Africa (3.5 percentage points) and the Caribbean (3.0 percentage points). In four of the nine regions the gap between the highest and lowest spenders has narrowed over the assement period. In all of these cases the maxima reportd decreased-especially in the transition countries of Central Asia and Central and Eastern Europe-although in Latin America the large factors in the reduction of variation within the region were the increases reported at the lower end of the scale.

Care needs to be taken in interpreting these results, for example, when attempting to draw conclusions about high levels of expenditure relative to GNP. It is true that they may be associated with high ratios of enrolment or low pupil-teacher ratios, smaller classes or relatively more contact hours between pupils and teachers—all of which are generally regarded as desirable features and likely to encourage the provision of good quailty education. Yet high levels of expenditure can occur even where enrolment rates are relatively low or pupil teacher ratios are relatively high and require further analysis in order to interpret and understand the underlying causes and reasons.

There remains a need to supplement the indicators used here with statistics which would make it possible to better capture and understand the variations covered in this summary analysis. The development of associated methodologies for analysis will make it possible in future to enrich understanding of the financing of education throughout the world.

II—Public current expenditure on primary education per pupil as a percentage of GNP per capita (Indicator 7b)

Response rate : 67 countries (time series)

This indicator measures the average cost of a pupil in primary education in relation to the theoretical average income of individuals in each country. It is a proxy measure of a country's ability to afford to pay for education and avoids problems of international comparability that result if expenditures need to be converted to a common currency.

In 1998, the regional average (median) expenditure per pupil varied between 8 per cent and 20 per cent of GNP per capita in the eight regions for which data are available compared with between 6 per cent and 19 per cent in 1990. All but one region - Central Asia - showed increases in the median values reported over the assessment period indicating that expenditure per student had increased relative to GNP per capita. This may have been the result of real increases in expenditure per pupil or decreases in GNP per capita or a combination of both. Nevertheless, in relative terms, the results suggest that countries have given a higher priority to funding allocated to primary education over the assessment period.

As with Indicator 7a, greater variations were reported within regions than between regions. For six of the eight regions for which data are available for Indicator 7b, the variations within regions widened over the assessment period. In the other two regions-Central Asia and South and Western Asia-the gap narrowed considerably but largely because of very large decreases in the highest reported values down from 37 per cent to 16 per cent in Central Asia and from 28 per cent to 15 per cent in South and West Asia (Table 3.8).

Figure 3.22 — Public current expenditure on primary education as a percentage of GNP, 1990 and 1998 (median values and variation within regions)

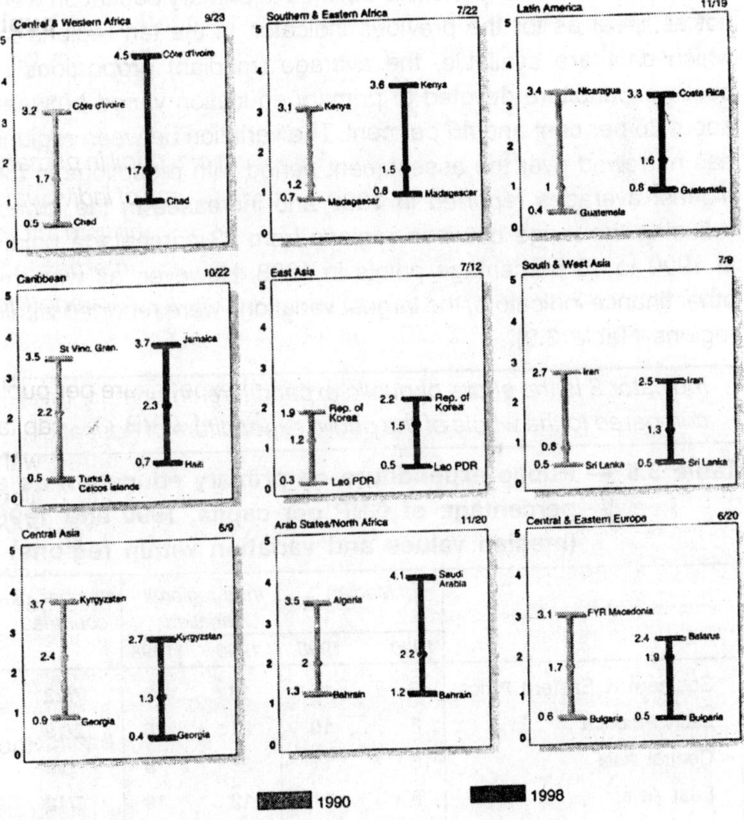

3 countries were added to the EFA data from the UIS database.

2 regions are not included in this graph, as the number of reporting countries (5 in total) is too few.

III—Public expenditure on primary education as a percentage of total public expenditure on education (Indicator 8)

Response rate : 89[5] countries (time series)

This indicator measures the relative priority given to primary education within overall public expenditure on education.

In 1998, the regional variations reported in the proportions of public education expenditure devoted to primary education were not as great as for the previous indicator. In the ten regions for which data are available, the average (median) proportions of public expenditure devoted to primary education varied between about 36 per cent and 46 per cent. The variation between regions has narrowed over the assessment period with reductions in the highest averages reported in 1990 and increases in the lowest reducing the range between regions from 23 percentage points in 1990 to 10 percentage points in 1998. However, as with the other finance indicators, the largest variations were reported within regions (Table 3.9).

Indicator 8 is the share of public expenditure on primary level compared to the whole of the public expenditure of education.

Table 3.8 — Public expenditure on primary education as a percentage of GNP per capita, 1990 and 1998 (median values and variation within regions)

	Median		*Intra-regional variation*		*Number of countries*
	1990	*1998*	*1990*	*1998*	
Southern & Eastern Africa	6	13	13	13	7/22
Latin America	8	10	21	26	12/19
Central Asia	16	11	25	9	6/9
East Asia	8	11	12	19	7/12
South & West Asia	7	8	24	10	6/9
Caribbean	12	16	11	18	8/22
Arab States/North Africa	19	20	21	32	10/20
Central & Eastern Europe	14	17	12	13	6/20

Table 3.9 — Public expenditure on primary education as a percentage of total public expenditure on education, 1990 and 1998 (median values and variation within regions)

	Median		*Intra-regional variation*		*Number of countries*
	1990	*1998*	*1990*	*1998*	
Central & Western Africa	49	46	61	36	11/23
Southern & Eastern Africa	34	42	23	25	7/22
Latin America	40	47	53	51	13/19
Central Asia	26	36	36	34	6/9
East Asia	41	43	64	35	6/12
South & West Asia	43	44	49	45	7/9
Caribbean	47	46	37	36	11/12
Arab States/North Africa	47	43	62	46	14/20
Central & Eastern Europe	39	44	66	60	7/20
Pacific	40	36	50	57	7/14

One region is not included in this table as the number of reporting countries, (2 in total) is too low

One country was added from the UIS database to complete the EFA data.

TEACHER QUALIFICATIONS

I—Percentage of primary-school teachers having the required academic qualifications (Indicator 9), and

II—Percentage of primary-school teachers who are certified to teach according to national standards (Indicator 10)

Response rate[6] : 83 countries (one or both indicators at least for 1998).

Both indicators are measures of the general quality of the teaching staff available within primary schools although neither takes account of competencies gained by teachers through their professional experience or self-instruction. Nor do they take account of other factors such as the working experience or status of teachers, teaching methods or materials, or the prevailing conditions in classrooms, all of which may affect the quality of teaching offered. High proportions of qualified and trained teachers are generally expected to indicate teaching forces which are well-equipped academically and have the necessary pedagogical skills to pass on knowledge effectively to pupils and hence to improve their scholastic performance. Since both indicators are based on minimum national qualification and training standards, care should be taken in comparing countries as these standards may vary greatly.

One-third of responding countries reported that all of their primary teachers had at least the minimum academic qualifications required to teach in primary education in their countries and eleven of these reported that their teachers had all received the minimum teacher training required. In some cases this may be because the two standards are in fact the same. Nevertheless, the qualification rates of teachers reported were often, but not always, higher than the proportions of teachers who had been trained. Some countries indicated in their narrative reports that in order to meet the increasing demand for teachers in line with the rise in primary school enrolment rates, they had placed a higher priority on recruiting staff with relevant academic qualifications, rather than expanding the teacher-training provision within their countries.

> *Indicator 9 measures the percentage of primary school teachers with at least the minimum academic qualifications required by the national public authorities for teaching in primary education. These qualifications are specified by the national authorities of each country and, of course, vary from country to country and may or may not be specific teaching qualifications. Indicator 10, on the other hand, measures the percentage of primary school teachers who hold teaching certificates indicating that they have received the minimum organised teacher-training normally required in that country to teach in primary education.*

In almost all regions of the world the median proportions of teachers with the requisite qualifications were in excess of 90 per cent; the exception was in South and West Asia where it was 82 per cent. The median proportions of teachers reported to have

Figure 3.23 — Percentage of primary school teachers qualified or trained to teach by region, 1998

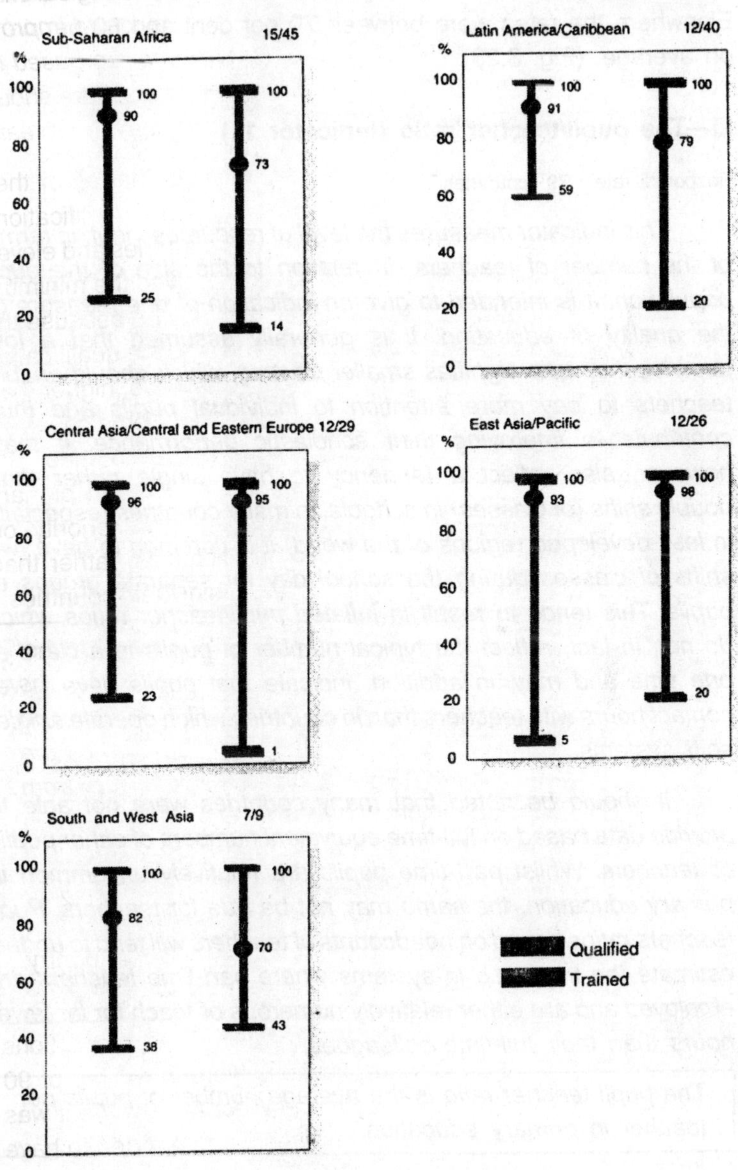

received the minimum training required were around the same levels in three of the regions for which data are available: Central Asia, Central and Eastern Europe, and East Asia and the Pacific. Elsewhere the rates were between 70 per cent and 80 per cent on average. (Fig. 3.23)

III—The pupil/teacher ratio (Indicator 11)

Response rate : 79[7] countries

This indicator measures the level of resources input, in terms of the number of teachers, in relation to the size of the pupil population. It is intended to give an indication of one measure of the quality of education. It is generally assumed that a low pupil/teacher ratio signifies smaller classes, which should enable teachers to pay more attention to individual pupils and thus contribute to improving their scholastic performance. It may, however, also reflect a tendency to have single rather than double shifts (of classes) in schools. In many countries (especially in less developed regions of the world) it is common to have two shifts of classes during the school day for separate groups of pupils. This tends to result in inflated pupil/teacher ratios which do not, in fact, reflect the typical number of pupils in a class at one time and may, in addition, indicate that pupils have fewer contact hours with teachers than in countries which operate single-shift systems.

It should be noted that many countries were not able to provide data based on full-time equivalent numbers of either pupils or teachers. Whilst part-time pupils are relatively uncommon in primary education, the same may not be true for teachers. Pupil teachers ratios based on headcounts of teachers will tend to under-estimate the true ratio in systems where part-time teachers are employed and are either relatively numerous or teach for far fewer hours than their full-time colleagues.

The pupil teacher ratio is the average number of pupils per teacher in primary education.

Figure 3.24 — Pupil/teacher ratio, 1990 and 1998 (median value and variation within regions)

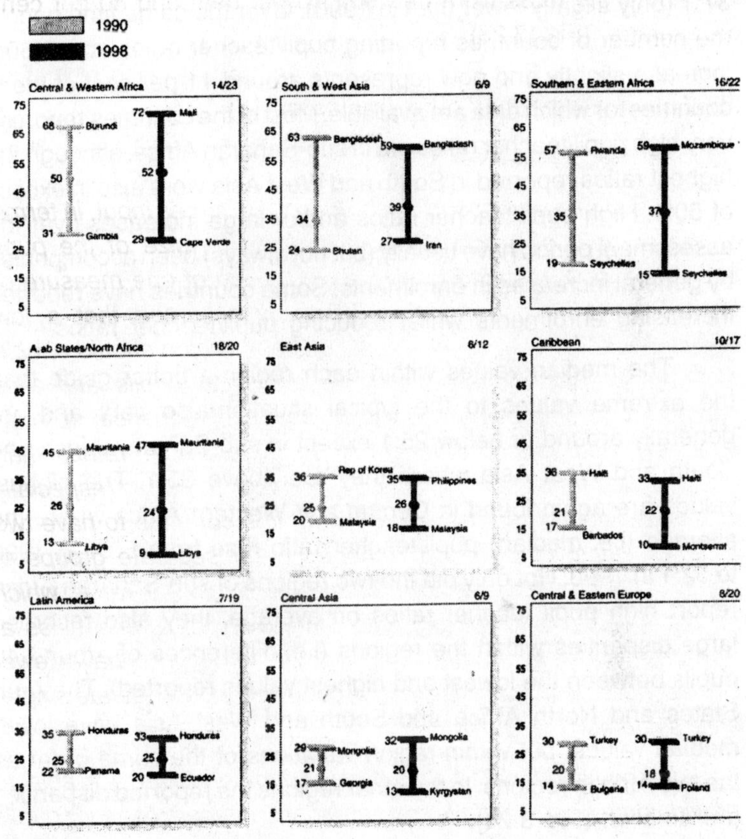

Supplementary data from 22 countries are included.

2 regions were not included as the number of responding countries (8 in all) was too few

The pupil/teacher ratios reported by countries vary greatly throughout the world from a low of 9:1 to a high of 72:1. In 1998, three-quarters of countries reported pupil/teacher ratios below 37:1 (only slightly fewer than in 1990). Over the same time period, the number of countries reporting pupil/teacher ratios above 50:1 increase slightly and now represents around 11 per cent of those countries for which data are available. Most of the countries reporting very high pupil/teacher ratios are in sub-Saharan Africa, although the highest ratios reported in South and West Asia were also in excess of 50:1. High pupil/teacher ratios and/or large increases over the assessment period have usually (but not always) been accompanied by general increases in enrolments. Some countries have reported increasing enrolments whilst reducing pupil/teacher ratios.

The median values within each region-a better guide than the extreme values to the typical situation-also vary and are generally around or below 25:1 except in sub-Saharan Africa and South and West Asia where they are above 35:1. The highest values are again found in Central and Western Africa where the average (i.e. median) pupil/teacher ratio rose from 50:1 in 1990 to 52:1 in 1998. Not only did the two regions of sub-Saharan Africa report high pupil teacher ratios on average, they also recorded large disparities within the regions (i.e. differences of around 40 pupils between the lowest and highest values reported). The Arab States and North Africa and South and West Asia have lower median values, but within-region variations of the same order as the two African regions. In the other regions the reported disparities are smaller. (Fig 3.24).

In most regions the change in the median values over the assessment period was equivalent to only one or two pupils. South and West Asia reported the largest change from thirty-four pupils per teacher in 1990 to thirty-nine in 1998.

Provincial results: Gabon and China

In some cases, within-country variations are nearly as great as the variations within a region as a whole. This is the case for

Figure 3.25 — Pupil/teacher ratio by province in Gabon, 1998

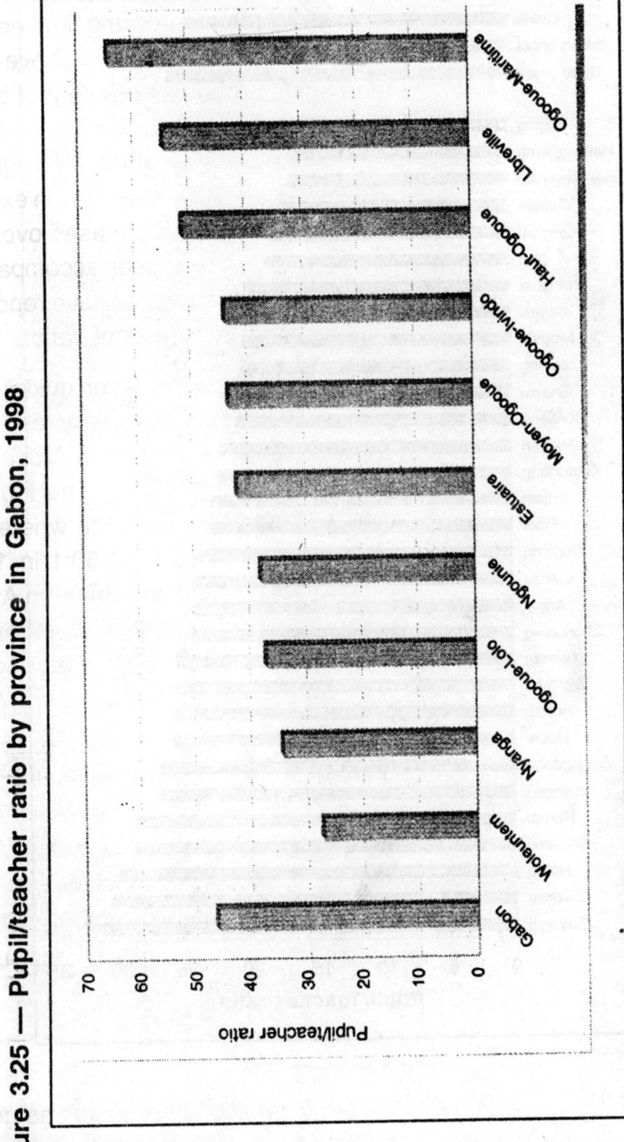

Figure 3.26 — Pupil/teacher ratio by province in Gabon, 1998

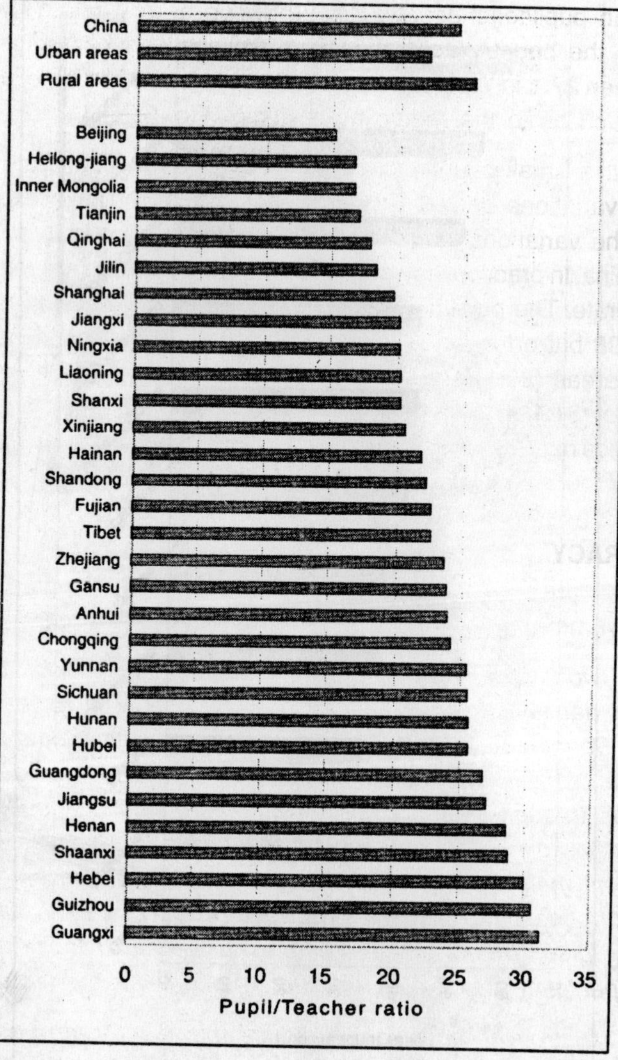

Gabon in Central and Western Africa. The pupil/teacher ratio for Gabon as a whole was 46:1 in 1998-some 6 pupils below the median pupil/teacher ratio for the region as a whole. However, within the country itself the provincial pupil/teacher ratios vary between 27:1 in Woluentem and 64:1 in Ogooue-Maritime, almost as much as in the region as a whole (Fig. 3.25).

If a small country such as Gabon has to cope with such wide variations between its provinces, we might have expected that the variations would be even greater in a country as large as China. In practice, however, the reported variations are relatively moderate. The pupil/teacher ratio for China as a whole was 24:1 in 1998 but on average was slightly less in urban (22:1) than in rural areas (25:1) and ranged from a low of 15:1 in Beijing to a high of 31:1 in Guangxi. Of course, these averages for each province may also mask much large within-province variations (Fig. 3.26).

LITERACY

The elimination of adult illiteracy (Indicators 16, 17 and 18)

Two groups of ages have been used in the study of literacy: young adults aged 15-24 years old; and adults aged 15 years and over. Countries collect these data in different ways. Some rely on household surveys, others collect the data concerning young people through school surveys, whereas others only collect the data through infrequent population censuses. Because of the different methodologies, the differences in sample coverage and the infrequency of some data collection, one must be cautious in interpreting reported literacy rates. In particular those near to 100 per cent may be an indicator of imprecise specification.

Most of the analyses by region and country are based on data provided in the EFA national reports. The global estimates and trends were drawn from recent estimates and projections of the UNESCO Institute for Statistics.

Literacy involves a continuum of reading and writing skills, often extending to basic arithmetic skills (numeracy) and life skills. Literacy reflects the accumulated achievement of primary education and adult literacy programmes in imparting basic literacy skills to the population, thereby enabling people to apply such skills in daily life and to continue learning and communicating using the written word. Because of the need to collect comparable data across the world, this rather complex concept is usually reduced to the definition : ***Literacy is the ability to read and write, understanding a simple statement related to one's daily life.*** *This is the indicator measured in the Education for All Assessment.*

General Analysis

The latest estimations and projections of the UNESCO Institute for Statistics show that four out of every five adults (aged 15 years and over) in the world are literate. The adult literacy rate continued to rise over the past thirty years, from 63 per cent in 1970 to 75 per cent in 1990 and to 79 per cent in 1998. At this rate of progress, it should reach approximately 83 per cent by the year 2010 (Fig. 3.27).

The number of adult literates in the world has more than doubled from an estimated 1.5 billion in 1970 to around 3.2 billion in 1998 (Fig. 3.28). Despite this progress, there were still some 880 million illiterate adults in the world in 1998, two-thirds of which were women (64 per cent). At the current rate of progress, it is estimated that the overall number will decrease to some 830 million by the year 2010, unless major efforts are made to improve the quality of basic education and eradicate illiteracy. More than 98 per cent of the world's adult illiterate population are found in the less developed regions.

Literacy rates among young adults (15 to 24 years-old) are generally higher than those for adults and have progressed from an estimated 74 per cent in 1970 to 84 per cent in 1990 and 86 per cent in 1998 (Fig. 3.27), bearing witness to efforts to improve the coverage and quality of education. However, despite such efforts, one out of every seven young adults is still illiterate.

Figure 3.27 — Trends in adult (15+) and young adult (15-24) literacy rate by region, 1970-2010

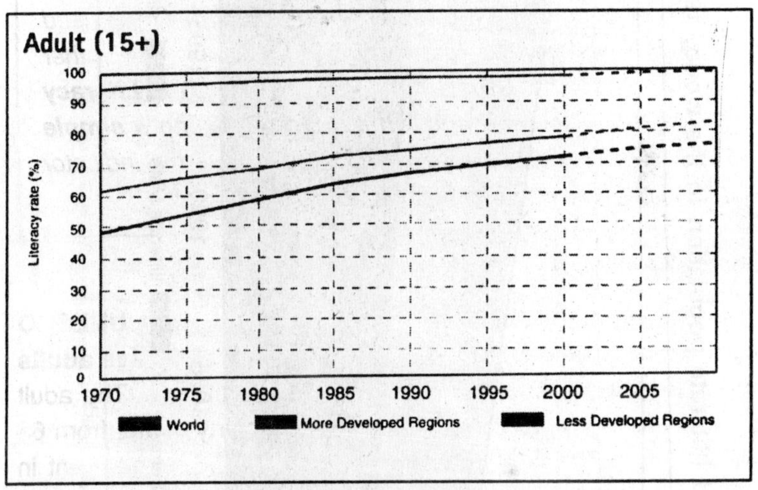

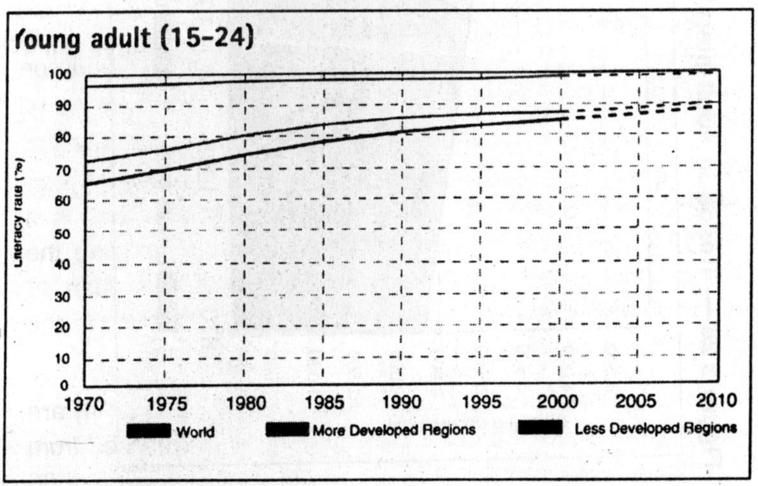

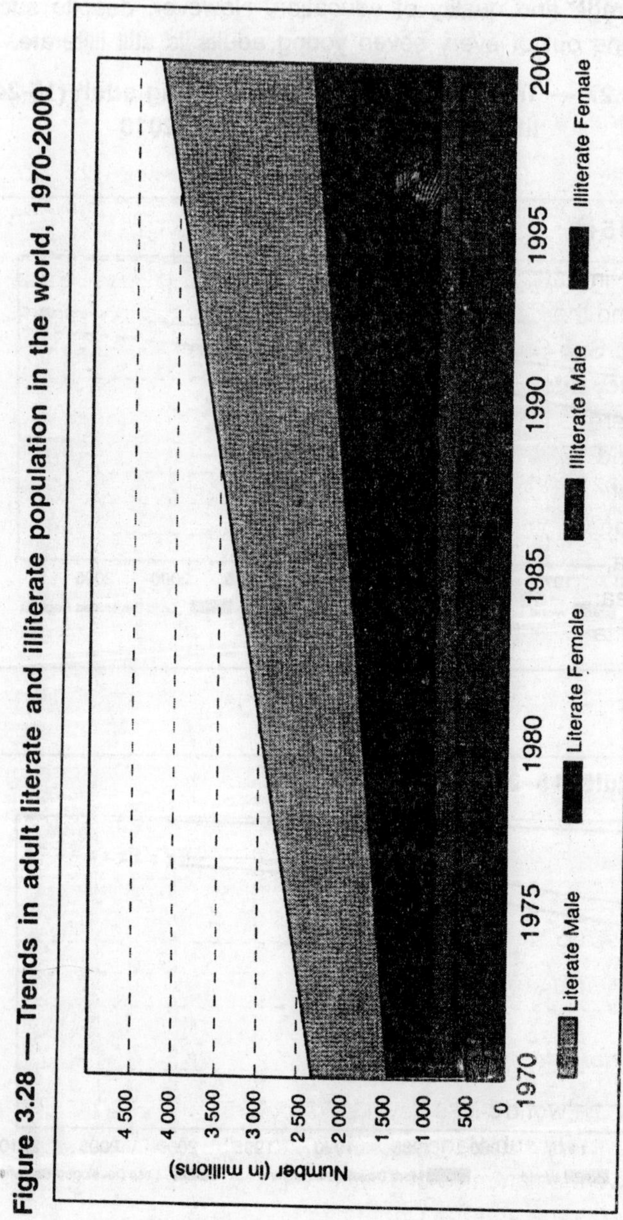

Figure 3.28 — Trends in adult literate and illiterate population in the world, 1970-2000

I—Literacy rate of 15-24 year olds (Indicator 16)

Response rate[8] : 80 countries

Regional analysis

According to the EFA National reports, countries in sub-Saharan Africa had a median literacy rate of 83 per cent, as compared to 95 per cent in the Arab States and North Africa, 97 per cent in Latin America and the Caribbean, 98 per cent in East Asia and the Pacific and nearly 100 per cent in the countries in transition. Sub-Saharan Africa, where there are still countries whose literacy rates are lower than 50 per cent, is also the region in which there is greatest variation between countries, followed by South and West Asia and the Arab States and North Africa with a variation between the minimum and maximum values of 61 percentage points. The largest disparities are observed in Central Asia, Central and Eastern Europe, Latain America and the Caribbean, and East Asia and the Pacific. All countries providing data over the decade reported an increase in literacy rates of varying degrees. The most dramatic change occured in Comoros, with a rise of 26 percentage points since 1990 (Fig. 3.29).

> *Literacy rate among the 15-24 years old has a special significance because it reflects the achievement of education systems over recent years.*

II—Adult literacy rate (Indicator 17)

Response rate[9] : 115 countries

Regional Analysis

Among the world's less developed regions, the adult literacy rate is the lowest in sub-Saharan Africa and South and West Asia, with respective median rates of 57 per cent and 58 per cent (Table 3.11). Latin America and the Caribbean and the Arab States and

North Africa have intermediate median rates of respectively 88 per cent and 80 per cent, and the highest can be observed in East Asia and the Pacific (94 per cent) and in Central Asia and Central and Eastern Europe (98 per cent). There are considerable inter-country disparities within each region. These disparities are highest in sub-Saharan Africa where the range extends from 25 per cent in Liberia to 88 per cent in Seychelles. This region is followed by Southern and Western Asia and the Arab States where inter-country disparities of 40 percentage points or more exist, Central Asia, Central and Eastern Europe and Latin America and the Caribbean experience the lowest disparities.

The adult literacy rate measures the percentage of the population aged 15 years and over who are literate.

For the majority of reporting countries, substantial progress was made in raising adult literacy rates over the decade, for example by a reported 21 percentage points in Bangladesh. However, progress is not universal as illustrated by the adult literacy rates in Honduras which dropped from 27 per cent in 1990 to 21 per cent in 1998.

Table 3.10— Literacy rates of population aged 15-24 years, 1998 (median value and variation within regions)

Region (number of countries)		*Median*	*Range*
Sub-Saharan Africa	(10)	83	61
Latin America/Carbbiean	(10)	97	9
Central Asia/Central and Eastern Europe	(11)	100	1
East Asia/Pacific	(9)	98	25
South and West Asia	(5)	67	40
Arab States/North Africa	(13)	95	31

Figure 3.29 — Literacy rate of the population aged 15-24 years old in some countries, 1990 and 1998

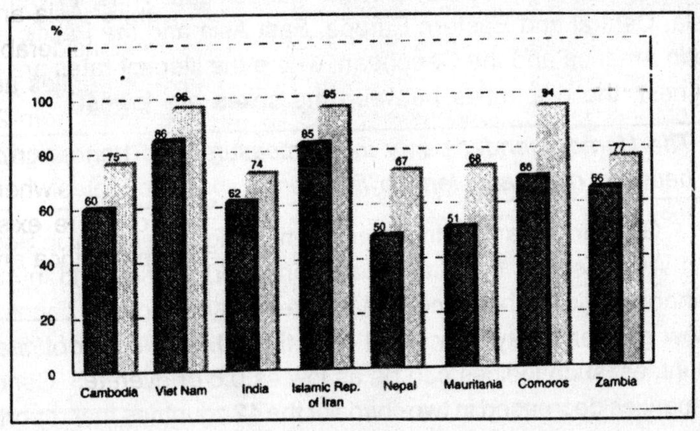

Table 3.11 — Literacy rates of population older than 15 years, 1998 (median value and intra-regional variation)

Region (number of countries)		*Median*	*Range*
Sub-Saharan Africa	(24)	57	63
Latin America/Carbbiean	(18)	88	28
Central Asia/Central and Eastern Europe	(14)	98	16
East Asia/Pacific	(10)	94	40
South and West Asia	(7)	58	54
Arab States/North Africa	(16)	80	79

III—Literacy gender parity index: ratio of female to male literacy rates (Indictor 18)

Response rate[10] : 78 countries for 1998

According to the latest estimation of the UIS, in 1990, there were eight literate women for every ten literate males and this rate saw only a slight improvement over the decade (Fig. 3.30).

Regional Analysis

In general, increases in overall adult literacy rates have been accompanied by reductions in the gender gap. Thus, in Central Asia, Central and Eastern Europe, East Asia and the Pacific and Latin America and the Caribbean, where the literacy rates are the highest, the disparities between the sexes are lowest.

> *The literacy gender parity index measures the gender gap between male and female literates.*

Gender disparities in literacy remain high especially in South and West Asia, in the Arab States and North Africa and in sub-Saharan Africa, where more than three-quarters of the countries show gender parity indices of less than 0.8. In some of these countries, such indices can be as low as 0.6 or even 0.5. Gender disparities decreased in two-thirds of the 42 countries that reported data on changes in literacy gender parity over the decade. For example, in Cambodia the literacy gender parity index increased from 0.52 in 1989 to 0.73 in 1997. Similarly increases have been observed in Yemen, Comoros, Mali, and the Islamic Republic of Iran, although these countries are still far from approaching gender parity in literacy (Table 3.12a).

The gender gap in literacy among young adults (15-24 year-olds) is generally lower than that of adults. Based on the data reported by 53 countries, there is little or practically no gender gap in literacy rates for the 15-24 age-group in the countries of Central Asia, Central and Eastern Europe, Eastern Asia and Pacific, and Latin America and the Caribbean. The widest gender disparities for young adults are found in South and West Asia, the Arab States and North Africa, and sub-Saharan Africa. In the latter region, the literacy gender parity indices in Liberia and Benin have been reported to be 0.54 and 0.52 respectively. However, in some countries, literacy gender parity deteriorated over the decade (Table 3.12b).

Figure 3.30 — Trends in the adult literacy rate by gender, 1970-2010

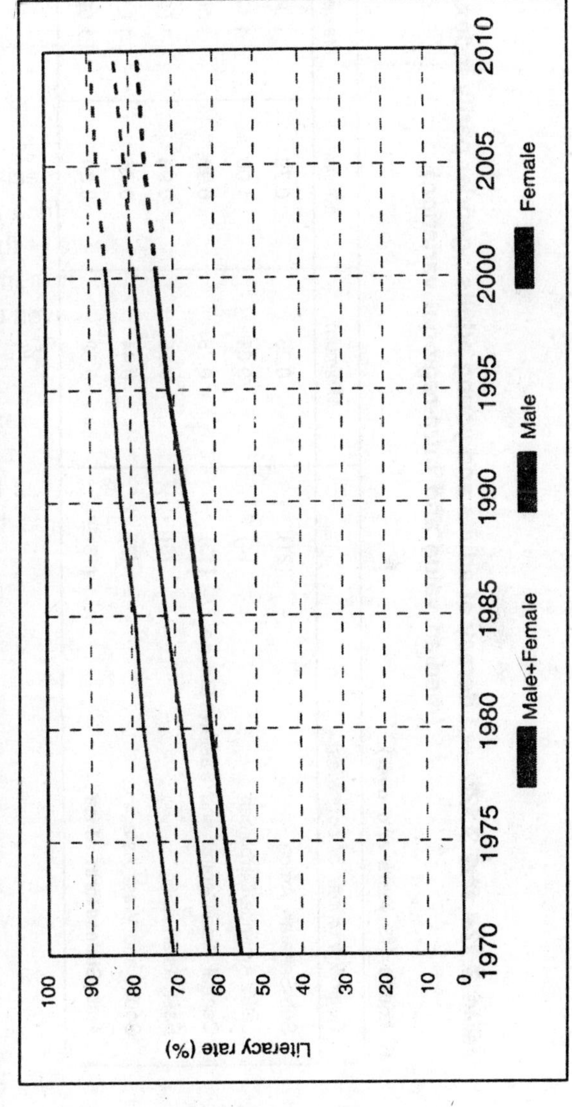

Table 3.12a and 3.12b — Literacy of adults and young adults : gender parity index, 1998 (median value and intra-regional variation)

a) Adults (15 years and over)

Region (number of countries)		*Minimum*	*Median*	*Maximum*
Sub-Saharan Africa	(21)	0.25	0.79	1.04
Latin America/Carbbiean	(14)	0.81	1.00	1.17
Central Asia/Central and Eastern Europe	(13)	0.79	0.99	1.00
East Asia/Pacific	(9)	0.65	0.98	1.02
South and West Asia	(7)	0.44	0.76	1.01
Arab States/North Africa	(13)	0.52	0.80	1.09

b) Young adults (15-24 years old)

Region (number of countries)		*Minimum*	*Median*	*Maximum*
Sub-Saharan Africa	(10)	0.52	0.91	1.05
Latin America/Carbbiean	(9)	0.97	1.00	1.09
Central Asia/Central and Eastern Europe	(11)	0.98	1.00	1.00
East Asia/Pacific	(6)	0.80	1.00	1.03
South and West Asia	(5)	0.64	0.71	0.95
Arab States/North Africa	(11)	0.67	0.99	1.02

REFERENCES

1. Some 136 countries provided information on early childhood programmes though of these only 46 provided a complete time series of data for the period of assessment. Thus the material in this section is based on between 46 and 136 countries, depending on the data item examined. Regional aggregations were calculated using EFA data for 110 countries and UNESCO Institute for Statistics data for 57 countries. There are no data for 27 countries.
2. 109 countries provided data on the apparent intake rates. Regional aggregations were calculated by combining the EFA data with UIS data for 54 countries. There were no data for 31 countries.
3. Regional aggregates were supplemented by UIS data—43 countries for indicator 5 (data unavailable for 9 countries) and 41 for Indicator 6 data unavailable for 27 countries).
4. 3 countries were added to the EFA data from the UIS database.
5. 1 country was added from the UIS database.
6. A further 16 countries have been excluded from this analysis because they reported data in a way which suggests that they regard their primary-school teachers as either qualified (Indicator 9) or trained (Indicator 10) but not both.
7. Supplementary data from 22 countries are included.
8. Of which 59 countries provided data for 1998, and 31 for 1990 and 1998
9. Of which 90 reported for 1998 and 55 countries provided time series data.
10. Of which 42 provided time series data.

APPENDIX I

THE SIX TARGET DIMENSIONS

1. Early Childhood Education and Care

Target: Expansion of early childhood care and developmental activities, including family and community interventions, especially for poor, disadvantaged and disabled children.

2. Primary Education

Target: Universal access to, and completion of, primary/basic education by the year 2000.

3. Learning Achievement and Outcomes

Target: Improvement of learning achievement such that an agreed percentage of an appropriate age cohort (for example, 80 per cent of 14 year-olds) attains or surpasses a defined level of necessary learning achievement.

4. Adult Literacy

Target: Reduction of the adult illiteracy rate (the appropriate age-group to be determined in each country) to, say, one-half its 1990 level by the year 2000, with sufficient emphasis on female literacy to significantly reduce the current disparity between male and female illiteracy rates.

5. Training in Essential Skills

Target: Expansion of provisions of basic education and training in other essential skills required by youth and adults, with programme effectiveness assessed in terms of behavioural changes and impacts on health, employment and productivity.

6. Education for Better Living

Target: Increased acquisition by individuals and families of the knowledge, skills and values required for better living and sound and sustainable development, made available through all education channels including the mass media, other forms of modern and traditional communication, and social, action, with effectiveness assessed in terms of behavioural change.

APPENDIX II

CORE EFA INDICATORS

Indicator 1 : Gross enrolment in early childhood development programmes, including public, private, and community programmes, expressed as a percentage of the official age-group concerned, if any, otherwise the age-group 3 to 5.

Indicator 2 : Percentage of new entrants to primary grade 1 who have attended some form of organised early childhood development programme.

Indicator 3 : Apparent (gross) intake rate: new entrants in primary grade 1 as a percentage of the population of official entry age.

Indicator 4 : Net intake rate: new entrants to primary grade 1 who are of the official primary school-entrance age as a percentage of the corresponding population.

Indicator 5 : Gross enrolment ratio.

Indicator 6 : Net enrolment ratio.

Indicator 7 : Public current expenditure on primary education a) as a percentage of GNP; and b) per pupil, as a percentage of GNP per capita.

Indicator 8 : Public expenditure on primary education as a percentage of total public expenditure on education.

Indicator 9	:	Percentage of primary school teachers having attained the required academic qualifications.
Indicator 10	:	Percentage of primary school teachers who are certified to teach according to national standards.
Indicator 11	:	Pupil teacher ratio.
Indicator 12	:	Repetition rates by grade.
Indicator 13	:	Survival rate to grade 5 (percentage of a pupil cohort actually reaching grade 5).
Indicator 14	:	Coefficient of efficiency (ideal number of pupil years needed for a cohort to complete the primary cycle, expressed as a percentage of the actual number of pupil-years).
Indicator 15	:	Percentage of pupils having reached at least grade 4 of primary schooling who master a set of nationally defined basic learning competencies.
Indicator 16	:	Literacy rate of 15-24 year olds.
Indicator 17	:	Adult literacy rate: percentage of the population aged 15+ that is literate.
Indicator 18	:	Literacy Gender Parity Index: ratio of female to male literacy rates.

APPENDIX III

KEY TERMS AND DEFINITIONS

Basic Education refers to a whole range of educational activities that take place in different settings and that aim to meet basic learning needs as defined in the World Declaration on Education for All (Jomtien, Thailand, 1990). It thus comprises both formal schooling (primary and sometimes lower secondary) as well as a wide variety of non-formal and informal public and private educational activities offered to meet the defined basic learning needs of groups of people of all ages.

Basic Learning Needs comprise both essential learning tools (such as literacy, oral expression, numeracy, and problem solving) and the basic learning content (such as the knowledge, skills, values, and attitudes) required by human beings to survive, to develop their full capacities, to live and work in dignity, to participate fully in development, to improve the quality of their lives, to make informed decisions, and to continue learning.

Coefficient of efficiency is a measure of the internal efficiency of an education system obtained by dividing the ideal number of pupil-years required for a pupil cohort to complete a level or cycle of education (e.g. the primary level) by the estimated total number of pupil-years actually spent by the same pupil cohort. The reciprocal of the coefficient of efficiency is the **input-output ratio.**

Compulsory Education refers to the number of years or the age-span during which children and youth are legally obliged to attend school.

Course is a planned series of learning experiences in a particular subject matter or set of skills, usually offered by an educational or training institution or programme for one or more pupils.

Crude birth rate: The CBR measures the frequency of childbirths in a population and represents the number of live births per 1,000 mid-year population.

Crude death rate: The CDR measures the frequency of deaths in a population and represents the number of deaths per 1,000 mid-year population.

Drop-out Rate is the percentage of pupils who drop out from a given grade or cycle or level of education in a given school-year.

Early Childhood Development (ECD) programmes offer a structured and purposeful set of learning activities either in a formal institution (pre-school) or as part of a non-formal child-care programme. ECD programmes generally focus on children from three years of age and include organised learning activities that constitute not less than 30 per cent of the overall programme of care. For purposes of the Assessment, ECD programmes should involve children for at least two hours per day and 100 days in a year. This would include, for instance, all pre-school programmes that conform to the ISCED Level 0 definition.[1]

Educational Institution has as its sole or main purpose the provision of education. Such institutions are normally accredited, or sanctioned, by some public authority.

Educational Personnel is a broad term covering three categories. Teaching staff are those persons who participate directly in instructing pupils (see Teaching Staff below). Other pedagogical and administrative personnel include headmasters, school administrators, supervisors, counsellors, school health personnel, librarians, curriculum developers, as well as educational administrators at the local, regional and central levels. Support personnel include clerical personnel, building operations and maintenance staff, security personnel, transportation workers, catering staff etc.

Educational Programme is a set of organised and purposeful learning experiences with a minimum duration of one school or academic year, usually offered in an educational institution.

Education System is the overall network of institutions and programmes through which education of all types and all levels is provided to the population.

Expenditures: Capital expenditures are for assets that last longer than one year. They include outlays for construction, renovation and major repairs of buildings and expenditures for new or replacements of heavy equipment and vehicles. Current expenditures are for goods and services consumed within the current year and which should be renewed if there is need for them the following year. They include emoluments such as gross salaries, plus non-salary compensation (fringe benefits). Gross salary means the total salary earned by employees, including any bonuses, extra allowances etc., before subtracting any taxes on employee contributions for pensions, social security or other purposes. Non-salary compensation includes expenditure by employers and/or public authorities for retirement programmes, health care or health insurance, unemployment compensation, disability insurance and other forms of social insurance, non-cash supplements (e.g. free or subsidized housing), free or subsidized child care and other such fringe benefits. Other current expenditures include those for contracted and purchased services and goods, such as: school books and other teaching materials, exercise books, and other supplies directly related to instructional activities; welfare services such as contracted and purchased services from outside providers related to school canteens, boarding schools, meals for pupils, school transport, medical services etc.; items of equipment not classified as capital, minor repairs, fuel, electricity, telecommunications, travel, insurance, services contracted from outside providers for the maintenance of school buildings, rents paid for school buildings and other facilities, as well as property taxes that educational institutions are required to pay in some countries, along with adjustments for changes (positive or negative) in fund balances in cases where the total funds received are not precisely equal to the total expenditures because the institutions have either added to or reduced their fund balances during the period in question.

Formal Education refers to education provided in the system of schools, colleges, universities and other formal educational institutions that normally constitutes a continuous 'ladder' of full-time education for children and young people, generally beginning at age five, six or seven and continuing up to 20 or 25 years of age. Formal basic education usually comprises than primary school grades, but may include also additional grades (e.g. lower secondary schooling) that are considered "basic". N.B. For purposes of the Assessment exercise, the term **Formal Basic Education** is used to distinguish cases where basic education in the formal school system is considered to extend beyond primary schooling.

Grade is a stage of instruction usually covered in one school year.

Graduate is a pupils or student who successfully completes a level of education, such as primary education.

Gross Enrolment Ratio (GER) is the total enrolment of pupils in a grade or cycle or level of education, regardless of age, expressed as percentage of the corresponding eligible official age-group population in a given school-year.

Infant mortality rate: The IMR is a measure of the probability of dying between birth and 1 year of age. It represents the annual number of deaths of infants under 1 year of age per 1,000 live births during the same period.

Life expectancy at birth: A widely used measure of the general level of mortality, this is the theoretical number of years a newborn will live if the age-specific mortality rates in the year of birth are taken as constant. It represents for a given year the sum of the mortality rates for all age combined.

Literacy is the ability to read and write with understanding a simple statement related to one's daily life. It involves a continuum of reading and writing skills, and often includes also basic arithmetic skills (numeracy).

Literacy Rate is the number of literate adults expressed as a percentage of the total adult population, 15 years of age or older.

Live birth: According to the standard definition of the World Health Organisation, this includes all births, with the exception of stillbirths, regardless of the size, gestation age, or "viability" of the newborn infant, or his or her death soon after birth or before the required birth-registration date. Only a few countries covered in this publication employed this concept, others relied on national concepts.

Net enrolment ratio (NER) is the number of pupils in the official school-age group expressed as a percentage of the total population in that age-group.

New Entrant is a pupil who enters primary education for the first time.

Non-formal education refers to any organised and sustained educational activities that do not correspond exactly to the above definition of formal education. Non-formal education may take place both within and outside educational institutions, and may cater to persons of all ages. Depending on country contexts, it may cover educational programmes to impart adult literacy, basic education for out-of-school children, life-skills, work-skills, and general culture. Non-formal education programmes do not necessarily follow the 'ladder' system, may have varying durations, and may or may not confer certification of the learning achieved.

Out-of-school children are those in the official school-age group who are not enrolled in school.

Pre-primary education (ISCED Level 0) refers to programmes at the initial stage of organized instruction, which are designed mainly to introduce groups of very young children, usually from age three or so, to a school-type environment, i.e.

to provide a bridge between the home and the school. Such programmes are variously referred to as infant education, nursery education, pre-school education or early childhood education. See also early childhood development programmes. In determining the boundary between simple childcare and pre-primary education or between pre-primary and primary education, the following criteria may be taken into account: the educational character of the programme; whether it is based at a school or specially equipped centre; staff qualifications; and the age-range of the children catered for. Pre-primary education generally aims at engaging groups of children in activities that encourage autonomy and enhance motor, cognitive and social skills, e.g. through stories, games, problem-solving, discussion, and building trustful relationship with other children and adults. Such programmes need to be distinguished from simple child-care programmes and day nurseries. A programme cannot be considered to belong to level 0 if it is aimed at children aged two years or less. The upper age limit depends on the entry age for primary education.

Primary education (ISCED Level 1), sometimes called elementary education, refers to educational programmes that are normally designed on a unit or project basis to give pupils a sound basic education in reading, writing and mathematics along with an elementary understanding of other subjects such as history, geography, natural science, social science, art and music. In some cases religious instruction is also featured. These subjects serve to develop pupils' ability to obtain and use information the children need about their home, community, country, etc.

The entry age for primary education usually varies between five and seven years. In principle, this level covers about six years of full-time schooling. In most countries, instruction in all subjects at this level is provided by a single teacher, whereas at Level 2 (lower secondary education), pupils may have several teachers, each providing instruction in a specific subject area. In countries with compulsory education laws, primary education generally constitutes the first (and sometimes only) cycle of compulsory education.

For countries were formal basic education extends up to eight years, which is often the duration of compulsory education, only the first stage should for comparison reasons, be included in Level 1. Normally, Level 1 should include only the first 6 primary years, so the remaining 2 or 3 years of basic education would be considered in Level 2. However, this distinction should be applied flexibly since it is recognised that while the allocation of pupils to Levels 1 and 2 is relatively straightforward, it is not so easy to allocate teaching staff, expenditures, etc. by level. See also 'Second Stage of Basic Education'.

Promotion rate is the percentage of pupils promoted to the next grade in the following school year. Some countries practice automatic promotion, meaning that all pupils are promoted, regardless of their scholastic achievement.

Public Educational Institutions are controlled, managed and operated by a public education authority or government agency or by a governing body (council, board, committee) most of whose members are either appointed by a pubic authority or elected by public vote. Most educational institutions are public, since they fall under the jurisdiction of the public education authorities. Various other public authorities may also be involved, such as the government services responsible for health, job training, labour, justice, defence, social services, etc.

Whereas **Private Educational Institutions** are not operated by a public authority, but rather are controlled and managed by a private body or have a governing board most of whose members are not selected by a public agency or elected by public vote. Private educational institutions may be operated by a non-governmental organisation or association, a religious body, a special interest group, a foundation, or a business enterprise, on either a profit or non-profit basis.

Public expenditure on education: This represents current and capital expenditures on education by local, regional and national governments, including municipalities. Household contributions are normally excluded.

Pupil is a young person who is enrolled an educational programme. For purposes of the Assessment, 'pupil' refers to a child enrolled in primary school, whereas children or adults enrolled at more advanced levels are **student.**

Pupil-year: is a non-monetary measure of educational inputs or resources. One pupil-year denotes the resources spent to maintain a pupil in school for one year.

Pupil Cohort is a group of pupils who enter the first grade of a level of education in the same school year and subsequently experience promotion, repetition, drop-out or successful completion, each in his or her own way

Pupil/Teacher Ratio (PTR) is the average number of pupils per teacher in a grade or cycle or level of education in a given school-year. In calculating pupil/teacher ratios, other educational personnel such as administrators and support staff are not taken into account.

Rate of natural population increase: This is the difference between the number of births and the number of deaths during a given year divided by the mid-year population. It excludes changes due to migration and may be either positive or negative.

Repeater is a pupil who is enrolled in the same grade for a second (or further) year.

Repetition Rate is the percentage of pupils who are enrolled in the same grade in the following school year as in the current school year.

Survival Rate is the percentage of a pupil cohort that enters together in the first grade of primary education and that reaches a given grade (e.g. Grade 5) or the final grade of an education cycle either with or without repeating a grade.

Second Stage of Basic Education, more commonly called **Lower Secondary Education (ISCED Level 2)** is typically designed to complete the development of basic skills and knowledge. In many countries, the educational aim is to lay the foundation for lifelong learning and individual development. The programmes at this level are usually on a subject-oriented pattern, requiring specialized teachers for each subject area. The end of this level often coincides with the end of compulsory education.

Special Needs Education refers to educational interventions and other support designed to address special learning needs. This term has come to replace the older term 'Special education', which referred mainly to the education of children with disabilities, usually in special schools or institutions. Moreover, the concept of 'children with special educational needs' now extends beyond those who have physical or other disabilities to cover also pupils who are failing in school for a wide variety of other reasons.

School-age population: number of children in the officially defined primary school age-group, whether enrolled in school or not.

Teachers are persons who, in their professional capacity, guide and direct pupils' learning experiences in gaining knowledge, attitudes and skills that are stipulated by a defined curriculum programme. A full-time teacher is a persons engaged in teaching for a specified number of hours per week according to official regulations in the country. A part-time teacher is one whose working load and associated financial remuneration are less than that of a full-time teacher.

Total fertility rate: An overall measure of fertility, this represents the theoretical number of births to a woman during her child-bearing years taking the given year's age-specific birth rates as a constant. It is calculated as the sum of the age-specific birth rates for all women of childbearing age.

Universal Primary Education (UPE) means full enrolment of all children in the primary school age-group, i.e. 100% net enrolment ratio.

REFERENCES :

1. ISCED = International Standard Classification of Education

APPENDIX IV

COMPOSITION OF REGIONS (A)

EFA REGIONS

Central and Western Africa (*23 countries*)

Benin, Burkina Faso, Burundi, Cameroon, Cape Verde, Central African Republic, Chad, Côte d'Ivoire, Democratic Republic of the Congo, Equatorial Guinea, Gabon, Gambia, Ghana, Guinea, Guinea-Bissau, Liberia, Mali, Niger, Nigeria, Republic of Congo, Senegal, Sierra Leone, Togo

Southern and Eastern Africa (*22 countries*)

Angola, Botswana, Comoros, Eritrea, Ethiopia, Kenya, Lesotho, Madagascar, Malawi, Mauritius, Mozambique, Namibia, Uganda, Rwanda, Sao Tome and Principe, Seychelles, Somalia, South Africa, Swaziland, United Republic of Tanzania, Zambia, Zimbabwe

North America and Western Europe (*26 countries*)

Germany, Andorra, Austria, Belgium, Canada, Cyprus, Denmark, Spain, the United States of America, Finland, France, Greece, Iceland, Ireland, Israel, Italy, Luxemburg, Malta, Monaco, Norway, Netherlands, Portugal, the United Kingdom, San Marino, Sweden, Switzerland.

Latin America (*19 countries*)

Argentina, Bolivia, Brazil, Chile, Columbia, Costa Rica, Cuba,

Dominican Republic, Ecuador, El Salvador, Guatemala, Honduras, Mexico, Nicaragua, Panama, Paraguay, Peru, Uruguay, Venezuela.

The Caribbean (*22 countries*)

Anguilla, Antigua and Barbuda, Aruba, Bahamas, Barbados, Belize, Bermuda, British Virgin Islands, Cayman Islands, Dominica, Grenada, Guyana, Haiti, Jamaica, Monsterrat, Netherlands Antilles, Saint Skitts and Nevis, Saint Lucia, Saint Vincent and the Grenadines, Suriname, Trinidad and Tobago, Turks and Caicos Islands.

Central Asia (*9 Countries*)

Armenia, Azerbaijan, Georgia, Kazakhstan, Mongolia, Tajikistan, Turkmenistan, Uzbekistan.

East Asia (*12 countries*)

Cambodia, China, Indonesia, Japan, Demoractic People's Republic of Korea, Republic of Korea, Lao People's Democratic Republic, Malaysia, Myanmar, Philippines, Thailand, Viet Nam

South and West Asia (*9 countries*)

Afghanistan, Bangladesh, Bhutan, India, Islamic Republic of Iran, Maldives, Nepal, Pakistan, Sri Lanka

Pacific (*14 countries*)

Australia, Cook Islands, Fiji, Kirbati, Marshall Islands, Nauru, Niue, New Zealand, Papua New Guinea, Samoa, Solomon Islands, Tonga, Tuvalu, Republic of Vanuatu

Arab States and North Africa (*20 countries*)

Algeria, Bahrain, Djibouti, Egypt, Iraq, Jordan, Kuwait, Lebanon, Libyan Arab Jamahiriya, Mauritania, Morocco, Oman, Palestinian Autonomous Territories, Qatar, Saudi Arabia, Sudan, Syrian Arab Republic, Tunisia, United Arab Emirates, Yemen

Central and Eastern Europe (*20 countries*)

Albania, Belarus, Bosnia and Herzegoniva, Bulgaria, Croatia,

Estonia, Federal Republic of Yugoslavia, Hungary, Latvia, Lithuania, Moldova, Poland, Romania, Russian Federation, Slovakia, Slovenia, Czech Republic, Turkey, the Former Yugoslavia Republic of Macedonia, Ukraine

E-9 (*9 countries*)

Bangladesh, Brazil, China, Egypt, India, Indonesia, Mexico, Nigeria, Pakistan

APPENDIX IV

COMPOSITION OF REGIONS (B)

WORLD REGIONAL CLASSIFICATION:

1. More developed regions

North America and Western Europe (minus Cyprus, minus Malta) Australia, Japan, New Zealand

2. Less developed regions

Sub-Saharan Africa
- Central and Western Africa
- South and East Africa

Latin America and the Caribbean
- Latin America
- The Caribbean

Eastern Asia and the Pacific
- Eastern Asia (minus Japan)
- Pacific (minus Australia and New Zealand)

South and Western Asia
- South and Western Asia

Arab States and North Africa
- Arab States and North Africa

Cyprus, Malta, Mongolia, Turkey

3. Countries in transition

Central Asia (minus Mongolia)

Central and Eastern Europe (minus Turkey)